GREATESTATES

How London's landowners shape the city

NLA, The Building Centre
26 Store Street
London WC1E 7BT

17 October — 19 December 2013

www.newlondonarchitecture.org/greatestates

This book is published by NLA to accompany the NLA exhibition
Great Estates: How London's landowners shape the city.

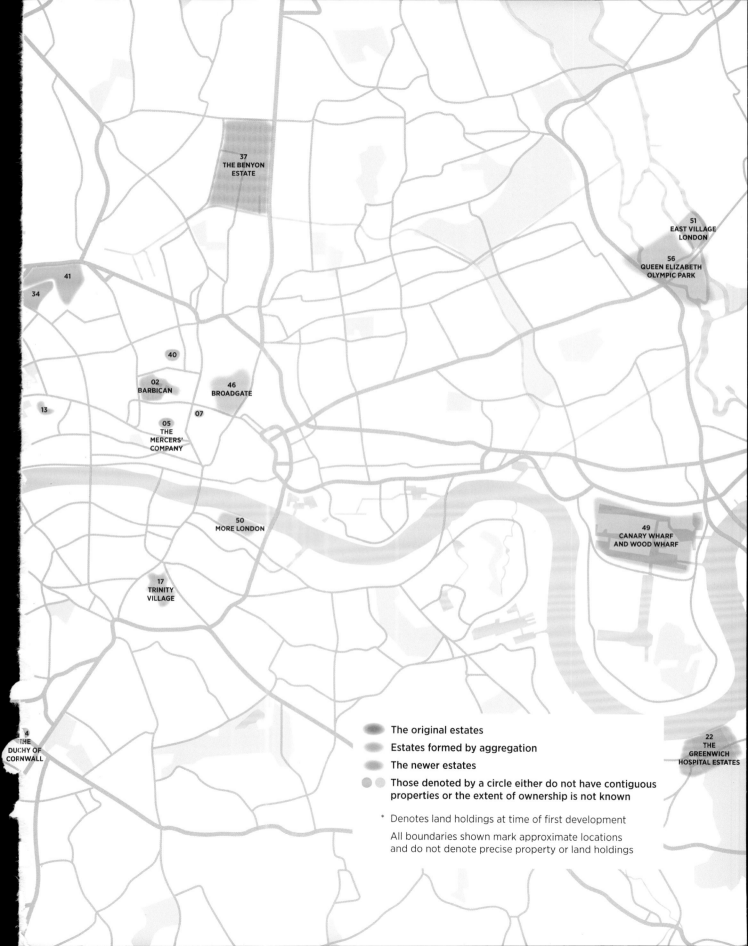

37
THE BENYON
ESTATE

51
EAST VILLAGE
LONDON

56
QUEEN ELIZABETH
OLYMPIC PARK

41

34

40

02
BARBICAN

46
BROADGATE

13

07

05
THE
MERCERS'
COMPANY

50
MORE LONDON

49
CANARY WHARF
AND WOOD WHARF

17
TRINITY
VILLAGE

4
THE
DUCHY OF
CORNWALL

22
THE
GREENWICH
HOSPITAL ESTATES

The original estates

Estates formed by aggregation

The newer estates

Those denoted by a circle either do not have contiguous
properties or the extent of ownership is not known

* Denotes land holdings at time of first development

All boundaries shown mark approximate locations
and do not denote precise property or land holdings

42 HAMPSTEAD GARDEN SUBURB

30 THE EYRE ESTATE*

12

54 KING'S CROSS

08

47 REGENT'S PLACE

19 THE BEDFORD ESTATES

33

11*

10

25 THE HOWARD de WALDEN ESTATE

02 TOTTENHAM COURT ROAD ESTATE

57 PADDINGTON CENTRAL

43

09 THE PORTMAN ESTATE

36 THE CHURCH COMMISSIONERS - HYDE PARK ESTATE

02 CONDUIT MEAD ESTATE

48

45

48

20 THE GROSVENOR ESTATE - MAYFAIR

18

01 REGENT STREET

05

52 COVENT GARDEN

14

48

03

31

01 ST JAMES'S

27 THE PHILLIMORE ESTATE

23

39

44 THE KNIGHTSBRIDGE ESTATE

20 THE GROSVENOR ESTATE - BELGRAVIA

53 VICTORIA

24 SOUTH KENSINGTON ESTATES

16 THE WELLCOME TRUST ESTATE

26 THE CADOGAN ESTATE

35 THE GUNTER ESTATE*

32

55 EARLS COURT

28*

MAP

CONTENTS

INTRODUCTION

INTRODUCTION

"Dined at my Lord Treasurer's, the Earl of Southampton, in Bloomsbury, where he was building a noble square or piazza – a little town..."

— The Diary of John Evelyn (9 Feb 1665)

London's 'little towns' – its distinctive neighbourhoods and urban villages – have made it unique among world cities. The sequences of streets, squares, parks, piazzas and gardens created by the estates, old and new, great and small, have evolved to create an enduring urban framework that supports and forms the backdrop to the economic, cultural and social life of the capital.

The estates' approach to making attractive places in which to live and work – and, perhaps most importantly, in maintaining and adapting them as such over a long period – has, in the past decade and more, been taken up by new projects seeking to regenerate large areas of the city. Where others come and go, the estates, with a commitment to long-term success, are stewards of a large part of London, but they have also shown a remarkable ability to evolve and innovate in one of the world's fastest-changing cities. The principles of placemaking that they have developed from centuries of expertise have proved highly influential.

How the estates evolved

London's unique quality as a patchwork of different neighbourhoods was ultimately driven by political and social agendas. The lack of an absolutist monarchy or overarching authority prevented the imposition of a grand vision dictated like that by Louis XIV in France in the 17th century and elsewhere in Europe. Instead, London as a city emerged from the piecemeal developments of self-contained estates under single ownership, which over time have meshed together physically and been overlaid by other patterns of planning, management and infrastructure, such as local authorities, public transport networks, and, most recently, the Greater London Authority.

Grants of land to aristocracy and gentry have, of course, been given by the monarch since the Conquest of 1066, and the Dissolution of the Monasteries in the 16th century resulted in major changes in the ownership of land previously held by the Church. Development on a large scale only took place after the Restoration of Charles II and accelerated after the Great Fire of 1666, when the wealthy wanted to escape the "impure and thick mist" of the crowded City of London (as Evelyn described it). The first estate in the modern architectural sense had been built in Covent Garden by the 4th Earl of Bedford in about 1631; he had employed Inigo Jones to lay out an Italianate arcaded square along with the church of St Paul's, creating a new model that revolutionised town planning in England.

New ideas of urban living – and using greenfields more profitably and ingeniously than for pasture – were encapsulated by a form of development that began with the Earl of Southampton's Bloomsbury Square. In 1661 the Earl gave out plots to builders on 42-year leases at low ground rents, on condition that the builder constructed houses – often at his own cost – that would ultimately become

the Market

1 Covent Garden Church. 2 King Street. *Covent Garden.* 3 James Street. 4 Russell Street.

Above: Aerial view of Bloomsbury Square, 1754. Courtesy of the London Metropolitan Archives

Above: View of Covent Garden from the south showing the market in the centre of the piazza, c1720. Courtesy of the London Metropolitan Archives

Right: Plan for the proposed construction of Regent Street, John Booth, 1818. Courtesy of the London Metropolitan Archives

the landlord's property. This introduction of the leasehold system, based on shared risk, ensured that the owner of the land benefited from development and a regular income from ground rent at minimal outlay to himself, while he retained ownership for the long term – sometimes a legal requirement as the land was often entailed or held in trust and so could not be sold.

The builder-cum-developer on his part also benefited by acquiring a prime site, and was often able to sublet individual plots. Most leases were fixed at 99 years, so within around three generations of ownership the estates were able, on reversions of leases, to renew them at increased rents or to redevelop the land.

Bloomsbury Square also initiated a new arrangement of town houses in terraces around garden squares, with servants and tradesmen located in mews or side streets. This pattern was adopted during the explosion of estate building that occurred around the turn of the 18th century, from which major estates such as Grosvenor, Portman and Howard de Walden emerged and which still largely shape the form of the West End of London today.

London emerged in the 19th century as a world powerhouse of industry and commerce, and its population more than quadrupled from 1 million in 1800 to 4.5 million in 1881. A second major wave of estate building, albeit quite different in form and supported by mortgaging on a massive scale, took place in the 19th century. New estates for the new affluent middle classes were developed in Kensington, Belgravia, Chelsea and other areas, while the arrival of the Tube, omnibuses and trams spurred growth on the outer reaches of west, north and south London.

The situation changed dramatically in the early to mid-20th century, when the impact of war damage, stagnant ground rents, and punitive death and estate duties adversely affected many of the well-established landed estates; many, including Portman, Bedford and Grosvenor, among others, sold large tracts of land, while other areas were subject to compulsory purchase for housing, education or other uses by public authorities.

The impact of leasehold reform legislation from the 1960s onwards and the right to buy freeholds has also irrevocably changed the shape of the estates, and stimulated greater diversification and the rise of a more professionalized, proactive approach to management. With significant changes in economics, markets and legislation in the last 25 years, Estates – even those created in that period such as Broadgate and Canary Wharf – have had to be nimble-footed enough to deal with change in order to survive.

Yet the estates have created an enduring legacy: some of London's most attractive, high-quality and distinctive neighbourhoods. But these are not merely historic artefacts – they continue to evolve, and the planning, design and management principles that made them so successful have provided a foundation for the regeneration of large brownfield sites, including King's Cross and the Queen Elizabeth Olympic Park. At the same time there is a realisation that majority ownership of areas that have already been developed can enable a much more effective coordinated management approach, which is the strategy employed by Shaftesbury PLC and Soho Estates, among others.

These emerging estates have identified and applied many core principles that helped the original estates flourish: mixed-use areas with a diversity of building types, leases and occupancy; facilities such as schools and health centres within walking distance; well-managed public realm and common amenities; strong community ties; and clear connections to adjoining neighbourhoods. The 'great estates' model continues to provide a flexible yet robust template that can inform new approaches to creating great places.

Left: Eaton Square,
The Grosvenor Estate

Left: Exchange Square,
Broadgate

Right: Carnaby Street facing
north, Shaftesbury PLC

Similarities and differences

By its nature of being embedded in one locality, each estate is different in character and form but some groupings emerge. The Bedford, Cadogan, City of London, Crown, Grosvenor, Howard de Walden and Portman Estates are the largest and longest-established estates and are often described as the traditional 'great' estates or 'original' estates. These estates were established in the 17th and 18th centuries and the urban landscape and management approaches they have initiated have influenced much future development. They are still evolving today.

In some cases, however, the shape of a historic estate in property terms has changed because of outside forces, in particular leasehold reform. This has totally recast those estates with the highest number of residential properties originally held freehold, for example the The Eyre Estate, as ownership has been fragmented. The estate retains a visual and architectural integrity, however, owing both to wider planning controls imposed at national or local levels, and estate management agreements or covenants that can impose restrictions on additions or alterations.

Over the past generation a new set of great estates for the 21st century and beyond has emerged. They comprise two main types: those such as Shaftesbury PLC and Soho Estates, which acquire land in the same area building up a large portfolio of frequently contiguous buildings; and those such as Canary Wharf, Broadgate and King's Cross which are mainly developing brownfield sites. The latter are largely a result of the 19th-century industrial legacy: large-scale industrial areas under single ownership, some highlighted by the London Plan as Opportunity Areas, which are developed as a coherent master plan. One of the most significant differences, however, between the original and most of the new estates is that the latter generally have direct ownership over public spaces, whereas in the former roads and streets have been adopted.

In legal terms, many of the older estates are held in trust for families or individuals; over time, depending on the original covenants, ownership may have devolved to several or even hundreds of people who are descendants of the original owners, or other institutions: The Colville and Pollen Estates are two such examples. This can make for a complex administrative structure in terms of generating returns for beneficiaries.

Other estates, including those held by City livery companies, are owned by charitable trusts or foundations, where revenue is often channelled into charitable giving or grants, or supporting educational foundations: until the 18th century it was not possible to set up a trust to see a charitable bequest fulfilled – to do so it was necessary to donate or bequeath land and/or property to an individual, the Church or a livery company. Some estates are also now publicly limited companies.

The role of estate managers and agents

Over the centuries estate managers and agents have played a significant role in the success of London's estates, and many firms including Cluttons, Savills, Deloitte Real Estate, Knight Frank and Farebrother continue to do so today. The history of some of these companies stretches as far back as the estates themselves: Cluttons, for example, was founded in 1765, and Savills in 1855. Traditionally, the agent was quite often the public face of the estate – walking its streets, meeting residents and inspecting properties.

Today, many of the larger estates, such as Cadogan and Grosvenor, among many others, employ their own extensive in-house teams to manage every aspect of the estate. Others, for example Pollen, Phillimore and Wellcome Trust, employ external management. This is done for a number of reasons, not least because such companies provide dedicated expertise in the management of property at a day-to-

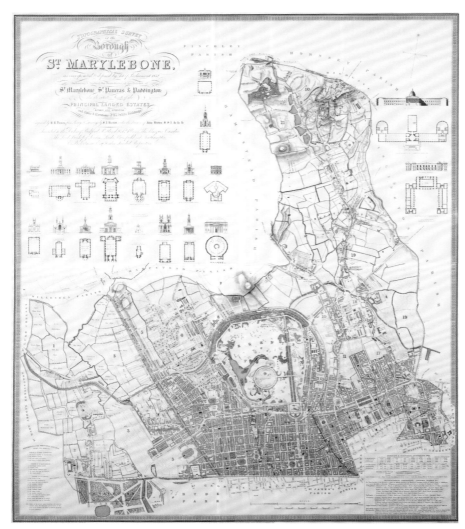

Left: St Marylebone map of 1834, drawn to show the landed estates within the Parish

day level that sometimes may no longer be held within an estate's owning family, trust or organisation. The legal structure of the estate, and its size and scale, can all have a significant impact on the decision to bring in external teams. An estate with many charitable trusts as beneficiaries such as the Mercers' Company, for example, can create a highly complex process of administration that can be time-intensive to manage internally. Other estates may in fact be large in terms of value or geographical area, but consist of lots of smaller individual units, and so again managing relationships with every occupier may be beyond the resources of the estate itself.

At one level, and in a time-honoured fashion, the manager or agent can be responsible for the hands-on approach to running the logistics of the estate on a daily basis: organising rent collection, dealing with tenants' or occupiers' queries, undertaking rent reviews and lettings, approving requests and assigning licences for alterations, providing valuations, and so on. Today, however, this is merely just one part of the manager's role. In a highly challenging and competitive market, all estates – whether managed internally or externally – need to ensure that the value of their portfolios is maintained and enhanced.

Where external managers are employed, they will also advise on strategic decision-making, for example by providing overviews of overall policy and trends in the property market, identifying parts of the estate that can be upgraded, unlocking value by restructuring leases, recommending areas for investment or properties to buy back to restore the integrity of the original estate, and other ways of maximising assets and capital. The external manager provides an independent viewpoint that can support building and managing relationships with occupiers, local authorities and other stakeholders. Good management remains at the heart of a successful estate: only a well-managed one will endure for the long term.

What makes an estate?

The success of the original estates is dependent on a number of key principles and tenets, many of which have, in the past decade especially, informed and been brought up to date by contemporary placemaking approaches:

Commitment to the long term

Good stewardship is the core tenet that underlies the management and ethos of the estates today. In practice this means that there is a commitment to managing the estate for the long term, to not only ensuring a viable revenue stream but also, today, to promoting London as a whole in a highly competitive international market. Stewardship is not just managing the estate effectively on a day to day level, but taking a creative, strategic approach that helps to sustain the right mix of uses and occupiers to embed long-term value.

Creating the urban framework

Ultimately, estates are masters at placemaking; underlying all successful original and contemporary estates is an approach that focuses on the masterplan and infrastructure rather than individual streets and buildings. As noted above, even the earliest estates were self-contained 'little towns': all the services that residents and workers needed, including housing, medical, educational and cultural facilities, could be found in one place – each estate had its own town hall, church or chapel, school, baths, etc built for the benefit of all. Focusing on the overall plan by setting a framework of appropriate scale, density and legibility meant that over time the estate was flexible enough to accommodate new uses, while the leasehold system allowed the owner to replace outmoded or redundant buildings when leases expired.

Left: Lloyd Square,
The Lloyd Baker Estate

Below: Connaught Street,
The Church Commissioners.
Photograph: Agnese Sanvito

It is this aspect which has perhaps been most influential in the creation of new parts of the city: the estate provides the 'framework' for the new place to emerge and acts as a catalyst for a real community to form. This holistic view was very important also in terms of looking at how new estates provide a 'complete offer' i.e. retail, commercial, leisure, services, etc. alongside the need for residential.

Familiarity with the local

In centuries past, and even today, the landowner lived on the estate itself and took personal pride in his or her property, while the owner's livelihood often depended heavily on the satisfaction of his or her tenants and occupiers. Ultimately the estate owner, and the agent where there was one, was intimately familiar with his or her property, and the best uses for it, and with the local community. This legacy is perhaps most apparent in the naming of streets and squares after family names, titles or landholdings that characterises so much of London's urban landscape today. Some estate owners made it their business to become acquainted with their tenants and their lives, in a paternalistic (or maternalistic) manner; Olive Lloyd Baker, for example, who owned the estate of that name in north London until her death in 1975, was often seen visiting her tenants, and "took an equal interest in their budgerigars … and aunts in Australia, though she often found it difficult, after consuming spaghetti at four in the afternoon … to do justice to tea and muffins in each of three adjacent houses" (*Survey of London*, vol 47, 2008). As Simon Jenkins has noted (in *Landlords to London*), "the strength lay in the identity of interest between the convenience and self-esteem of the residents and the long-term viability of the estate itself".

Today many traditional estates value the direct connection and personal relationships that they or the owning family have with their occupiers, customers and tenants. This is seen also in the long-standing tradition of directing funds for charitable, educational, artistic and welfare initiatives at a local level. This relationship has also moved with the times by more and better use of new technology and communications, including web, social media, and community events, to stimulate new interest as well as to support the local community. Branding has become more apparent in promoting particular areas of a estate. Many estates have developed distinct 'brand identities' including Marylebone Village (by Howard de Walden), Portman Village (by Portman) and the Hyde Park Estate (by The Church Commissioners), among many others.

Employing a holistic and proactive management approach

The original estates have proved extraordinarily adaptable to change, and over time have provided a framework that has helped to sustain London's economic, cultural and social activity. Through the benefit of retaining assets in single ownership, and an imperative to sustain value in the long term, estates have taken an organic and holistic approach to renewal and development.

There has been a continuous process of managing properties over the short, medium and especially long term through their lifecycle in order to maximise the value of the asset: letting, buying back or reversion, refurbing and then reletting. Historic and architecturally significant buildings are restored and maintained to retain their long-term value both individually and for the character of the estate, but also to ensure that they can be adapted to new uses. In some cases, where long leases exist, an estate freeholder can proactively decide to leave the property as it is and redevelop it in the future; decision-making can often be more considered.

On the other hand, a longer-term approach that is not dependent on immediate commercial gain allows estates to use exemplar projects or refurbishment of particular buildings and public spaces to regenerate a wider area; this can support uplift both elsewhere on the estate and beyond it. Similarly, estates are fundamentally mixed-use and a priority has been to implement and continuously evaluate a diverse tenant mix strategy to both create distinctive destinations and environments, especially in those estates where retail use is predominant. Alongside this, estates have become much more involved in developing innovative public realm strategies in order to maintain a high-quality, attractive context. Promotion and management of the place rather than the owner is one of the most important key principles – through long association with an area, estate owners and managers have an intimate knowledge of and association with it and a mission to retain and promote its distinctive character and spirit: Soho Estates' mission, for example, is to 'keep Soho's soul'.

Challenges for estates
Estates continue to face a range of challenges, politically, economically, socially and legally.

Legislation
Leasehold reform and the right to buy freeholds have presented a major challenge for estates, especially those with large areas of residential properties, and have resulted in some cases in the fragmentation of some of the original estates. The Leasehold Reform Act of 1967 was the first to allow lessees of smaller houses to buy the freehold of their properties, and this was extended in in 1974. Clauses in the Leasehold Reform, Housing and Urban Development Act in 1993 meant that owners of even the largest houses were able to enfranchise. Many estates have been legally obliged, therefore, to sell freeholds, sometimes on a large scale, resulting in a dramatic shrinking of the holdings as the estate moves out of single ownership. On the other hand, the capital generated from sales – mostly in the case of the larger estates – has allowed them to reinvest elsewhere and to initiate major works such as public realm improvements. Future rent policy and welfare benefit reforms are a particular challenge for organisations such as Peabody which are focused on social/affordable housing, but also for all estates that seek to sustain a mix of uses and occupation.

Economic competition
To maintain its international profile as a leading world city London as a whole have to vie with Paris, Milan, New York and others. Estates, both original and contemporary, are taking the lead in encouraging the emergence of new retail and leisure destinations and commercial hubs in order to attract new interest and to respond to ever-changing tastes, demands and expectations in a highly competitive global market. At street level this can involve maximising uses within buildings in order to create a more efficient use of space, as well as continuous research into new trends, and, as noted above, a much more brand-conscious approach. Some estates with an international portfolio have also taken the step of replicating their approach in their holdings abroad: in Vancouver, Canada, for example, Grosvenor has been acquiring land in Ambleside Village, with the aim of revitalizing this neighbourhood through a major scheme involving new retail and residential space, along with public art and cultural facilities.

Maintenance
Most original estates are either wholly or largely within conservation areas and have a very high proportion of listed buildings. Historic assets are also an important

part of the character of many contemporary estates, for example King's Cross. However, refurbishment and maintenance require considerable amounts of capital, and can be a continuous process, especially as leases expire in phases. With layers of development built up over time, each street or even building can be different, and require a bespoke approach.

A big challenge is also presented by upgrading historic and listed buildings in order to meet new energy efficiency minimum standards, especially at a district-wide level, and also the integration of fibre optics, Wi-Fi networks and IT infrastructure to meet business and residential demand.

What lessons do estates have for us?

The great estates have been responsible for the creation of high-quality places in London and their approach has been successfully reinterpreted to create new pieces of the city by developers and landowners, who have seen the benefits of researching how and why certain parts of London have continued to attract new residents, workers and visitors. As Design Council Cabe notes, 'given that they are a still a place where people love to live and work, the great estates can be a source of inspiration for designers today'. Some of the key principles are:

Control of the environment: retaining or acquiring ownership of all or majority holdings in a specific area or street enables a landowner to set and maintain high standards of quality not simply for their own gain, but for the benefit of all occupiers, visitors and users. Even where the long-term interest has been sold certain minimum provisions should be in place in terms of estate management to ensure quality and consistency of approach.

High-quality management: contemporary estates have learned from the original ones that having a locally based, on the ground management team that understands the area is second to none in maintaining good personal and business relationships with tenants and occupiers. Placemaking also means creating a balance of uses so that the whole is greater than the sum of its parts; maintaining an attractive, interesting and high-quality public realm is an equally important part of this approach.

Looking at the broader picture: a 'great estate' was not simply a collection of streets, buildings and open spaces – its social, cultural and economic aspects were integral to its success: traditionally, landowners looked beyond the physical to implement policies that addressed the need for housing, employment, education and entertainment in order to sustain a community over the long term and to reinforce their commitment to future generations.

Strategic masterplanning is the foundation: the estates have shown that where there are options and flexibility in phasing development over time and an option to accommodate new land uses according to market demand, demographic changes and external forces, places of lasting value in every sense can be created.

Long termism and placemaking

For some years economists have highlighted problems related to the short term nature of much corporate business, driven by quarterly earnings rather than long term value. The pressure to deliver quick results, to the potential detriment of the longer-term development of a company, has become an entrenched feature of the UK business environment. In the world of property, developers whose main interest is in disposing of stock rather than holding and managing it have little interest in how their products perform beyond the period of their responsibilities.

The original estates provide a masterclass in corporate long termism and sustainability for the new estates who recognise that management of their property is key to maintaining value over time. So you have British Land at Broadgate with a rolling programme of public space improvements to maintain the vitality and attractiveness of the estate; at King's Cross, right from the start of the masterplanning process, Argent committed to the long-term success of the area by recognising that stewardship had to be at its core. The legal agreement between Argent and its development partners LCR and Excel established a joint venture which specifically encouraged all parties to look to the long term, that would provide a structure to finance each phase of the development against the value of the land and any completed parts so that there would be no need to sell off the early phases in order to finance subsequent development or provide short-term returns. The agreement set out how the ongoing development would be owned – and managed – as a whole. It was recognised that it would be in the developer's interest to place an emphasis on quality, in design, construction, environmental management and long-term operation of the estate.

We recognise once again that the arrangement rather than the design of individual buildings is key to creating successful communities. While the Georgian Square is one of the most successful pieces of urban design ever invented and a key part of the character of London, it was also seen by its originators as a generator of sales. Samuel Cockerell, writing in 1790 to the governors of the The Foundling Hospital Estate recommending the construction of Mecklenburgh and Brunswick Squares, eloquently described the proposed squares as "principal features of attraction".

In estates today such features of attraction can be found in improvements as well as new building. The regeneration of Mount and Elizabeth Streets delivered by The Grosvenor Estate, of Regent Street by The Crown Estate, Marylebone High Street by Howard de Walden and Duke of York Square by Cadogan are stand out examples. In the development of Broadgate, Stuart Lipton's brief to his architect Peter Foggo of Arup Associates was for a sense of place – genius loci – that generally did not exist in the City of London at the time. As a result spaces like The Broadgate Circle and Exchange Square proved hugely popular in attracting tenants to the estate's buildings and office workers from the surrounding areas at lunchtime and in the evenings to create a vibrant new quarter. More recently the City of London Corporation have been upgrading public spaces in the Square Mile, turning streets into social spaces rather than routes for vehicular movement. At King's Cross, Granary Square is just the sort of feature described by Cockerell, creating a central focus for the estate.

When the architects Dixon Jones presented their designs for the masterplan of Chelsea Barracks to Qatari Diar, they perceived it as an estate in the tradition of neighbouring Grosvenor and Cadogan. The architects used Grosvenor's Mayfair, where all the original buildings have been replaced yet the ground plan remains the same, as a precedent for the strategy for change and renewal. Thus, while the buildings are renewed to meet the needs of contemporary occupiers, the squares and spaces – the features of attraction that create that elusive sense of place – remain.

Top: Granary Square, King's Cross
Above: Duke of York Square,
The Cadogan Estate

Queen Elizabeth Olympic Park,
with views to the city beyond

THE ESTATES

THE ORIGINAL ESTATES

These historic estates have set a pattern that operates effectively today and provides lessons for contemporary developers.

Founded: 1066*

The Crown Estate

The Crown Estate is arguably the oldest of the original London estates. It is unique in being owned by the Monarch in right of the Crown, that is by virtue of his or her holding that position rather than as an individual. The Crown Estate extends throughout Britain and comprises urban and rural estates, ancient forests, farms, parkland, coastline and marine holdings. It has significant ownership in London, the best known parts of which are Regent Street, around 50 per cent of St James's and properties in Regent's Park.

The origins of most of The Crown Estate date back to 1066, when William the Conqueror assumed control of all land in England 'in right of the Crown'. Over time, the Sovereign granted large areas of land to the nobility and sold others to raise revenue. By the accession of George III, in 1760, the Crown lands had been reduced and were producing relatively little income. An agreement was reached whereby the King accepted a fixed annual payment, in return for the effective surrender of the Crown lands for the duration of his reign, which would be managed on behalf of the Government, with the surplus revenue returned to the Treasury. Successive sovereigns have repeated this agreement at the beginning of each reign. Today the net surplus generated by the Estate goes to the Treasury for the benefit of the nation.

Managed under the terms of a 1961 Act, The Crown Estate Board has a duty to maintain and enhance the value of the estate and the return obtained from it, but with due regard to the requirements of good management. In the last decade the value of the property portfolio overall has grown from £4 billion to £8.1 billion. While the urban estate retains many historic and architecturally nationally important buildings, it is now mixed with offices, homes, shops, restaurants, hotels, retail parks, shopping centres, industrial parks and many more modern holdings.

In London The Crown Estate retains long-term ownership of 460 largely residential and institutional properties in Regent's Park and Kensington Palace Gardens comprising classical terraces and villas, designed by John Nash and Decimus Burton, among others. The Estate's residential holdings also include property near the South Bank, and in Eltham, Richmond, Egham and Hampton. The organisation is now more than halfway through a £1 billion investment plan for Regent Street to further build on its reputation as a world-class shopping and retail destination and has also begun a £500 million programme of investment to enhance and refine the properties in St James's, its other main central London location.

Regent Street is perhaps the best-known of The Crown Estate's assets in London, and its origins lie in the plans for development drawn up for the Prince Regent by the builder-architect John Nash in the early 19th century. Completed in 1826, it was to incorporate 'shops appropriated to articles of fashion and taste', and was the world's first purpose-built street dedicated to retailing. In the 1920s there was a complete

*Dates of foundation refer to the point at which the estate first acquired or assembled land and property in London

redevelopment of the street. Towards the end of the 20th century the initial building leases were expiring and the estate decided to initiate a rebuilding scheme that would give the street greater visual uniformity and meet modern occupiers' requirements.

While the 2km of street frontage has remained with its recognisable Grade II-listed facades, since 2002 the Regent Street Vision investment programme has been implemented, transforming the appeal of the location. It has, through 2 million sq ft of development behind the facades, created exemplary commercial, retail and visitor facilities together with the delivery of significantly improved public realm. Over the first 10 years more than half of the retail offering on the street has changed, so that in addition to some of the long-standing retailers in place, such as Burberry and Austin Reed, brands such as Apple, Banana Republic and Anthropologie have since joined the street. As well as retail, the regeneration has provided a range of varied office space, for international company headquarters for occupiers such as Apple and Telefónica Digital. Developments in Regent Street also include the addition of residential units. This regeneration has been carried out in partnership with Norges Bank Investment Management (NBIM) – Norway's $760 billion sovereign wealth fund.

The programme of public realm improvements has created two pedestrianised food quarters for workers and shoppers and closed several unappealing side streets for pedestrian access. The Crown Estate has been instrumental in helping deliver the transformation of Oxford Circus and Piccadilly Circus, the gateways to Regent Street.

The Regent Street programme is now well past the halfway point. The next developments to be completed at Block W4 (153–167 Regent Street) and Block W5 South (169–179 Regent Street), which together will deliver in excess of 150,000 sq ft of office and retail space, are already underway. The street in its third regeneration has won many national and international industry awards.

Right: St James's Gateway

In St James's – an area bounded by Trafalgar Square, Piccadilly Circus, Green Park and Buckingham Palace – The Crown Estate owns nearly 50 per cent of the properties encompassing some 4 million sq ft of retail, office and residential space with a value of over £1 billion. In 2012 it acquired the freehold interest in of Princes House for £87 million, which represented the only significant gap in its holdings on the northern side of Jermyn Street/southern side of Piccadilly. A long-term strategy is in place to protect St James's position as a distinctive and world-renowned high-end business district, with shops and restaurants, appropriate for the 21st century while retaining its architectural heritage.

Major redevelopment projects include St James's Gateway and St James's Market. The former, completed in June 2013, was the first delivered by The Crown Estate in partnership with a major international investor, Healthcare of Ontario Pension Plan (HOOPP). Designed by Eric Parry Architects the building offers 5,300 sqm (57,000 sq ft) of office space, 2,600 sqm (28,000 sq ft) of retail space and 1,670 sqm (18,000 sq ft) of residential space – confirmed occupiers include Tiger of Sweden, set to open its flagship London store on Piccadilly here. The scheme also makes an important contribution to St James's public realm through the transformation of Eagle Place and by introducing inspiring public art from Richard Deacon, Turner Prize winner, and Stephen Cox.

The St James's Market project is a £320 million scheme delivered in partnership with Oxford Properties, a Canadian investor, and will provide a new public square, offices and retail directly south of Piccadilly Circus. Designed by Make, it is intended to create a new destination on the neglected site of St James's Market. The Regent Street block will be redeveloped behind retained facades; the Haymarket block will be replaced with a high-quality, contemporary office and retail building in line with the quality, scale and materials of the surrounding area. Public realm improvements include the provision of a 950 sqm pedestrian square. Much of the newly configured site will be traffic-free and transformed into thoroughfares which improve connectivity and the site's relationship with the wider urban context.

www.thecrownestate.co.uk; www.regentstreetonline.com; www.stjameslondon.co.uk

Right: Quadrant 3
Below: Regent Street W5, view from rooftops © AHMM

Founded: 1067
(based on earlier Saxon records)

The City of London Corporation

The City is the oldest part of London, established by the Romans as 'Londinium' in about AD 50, soon after their invasion of Britain. In 1067, one year after his victory at the Battle of Hastings, William the Conqueror granted the City the right to the freedoms and independence its citizens had enjoyed under Edward the Confessor; this charter remains the basis of many City privileges.

The property holdings of The City of London Corporation are among the oldest and most diverse of the original London estates. The position of City Surveyor dates back to 1478 and the current incumbent is the 34th to hold this post. The City's estates are divided into three main parts: the City Fund, City's Estate (part of the endowment fund known as City's Cash) and the Bridge House Estates. In total the investment and operational property interests extend by over 22 million sq ft, comprised of 1,240 main properties.

Income generated from properties held as part of the City Fund, mostly within the City boundaries, supports the Corporation's activities as a local authority, police authority and port health authority. One of the main City Fund areas is the Barbican Complex, the City's largest residential estate, which also includes the City of London Girls' School, Guildhall School of Music and Drama and Museum of London, along with Europe's largest multi-venue arts centre. Situated over 40 acres on the northern edge of what was once the Roman City (surviving parts of the old London Wall are visible), this Grade II-listed complex is now recognised as a classic of modernist architecture, and was built from 1965 to 1976 on an area almost entirely destroyed by bombing in World War II. It was designed by Chamberlin, Powell and Bon, who were also responsible for the Golden Lane Estate to the north (also part of the complex; built 1957–62). While many residential long leases in the Barbican have been sold, the City continues to manage public spaces and services on the estate, and its recent investment – such as the creation of two new cinemas, and the redevelopment of Milton Court as a residential tower with performance and teaching facilities including a 625-seat concert hall – seeks to reinforce the Barbican's international reputation as a cultural hub and its links to creative and cultural industries on the northern City fringes.

The City's Estate, an endowment fund built up since the 13th century, is a privately held estate comprising land and property either acquired under royal charter through the Royal Contract of 1628 – by which Charles I granted the City a number of estates in Crown ownership in repayment of loans – or bequeathed to the City by dignitaries and citizens. The fund is now used to finance activities mainly for the benefit of London as a whole, including all of the Lord Mayor's activities; the maintenance of the Guildhall, Mansion House and Smithfield, Billingsgate and Leadenhall Markets; and the upkeep of four schools. The City's Estate also supports the management and conservation of more than 10,000 acres of open space across London and beyond, including Hampstead Heath, Burnham Beeches and Epping Forest, some parts of which have been owned since 1870. Most of the City's estate properties are in the City, West End, Bloomsbury and Islington.

Smithfield Market (London Central Markets) is the only wholesale market that remains on its original site within the City. Livestock and meat have been traded here – on a site described in 1174 as a 'smooth field' – for more than 800 years. The City gained market rights under a royal charter granted in 1327. In 1860 it obtained an Act of Parliament permitting the construction of new buildings on the site. Work began in 1866 on the two main sections, the East and West Buildings, built above newly built railway lines connecting London to every other part of the country and completed in 1868. Further buildings were added – the General Market in 1883 and the Annexe Market in 1888. Since 2010 Henderson Global Investors has

Above: Proposed view for Smithfields, designed by John McAslan + Partners

been working with the City on a conservation-based, mixed-use scheme (Smithfield Quarter), designed by John McAslan + Partners, for the General Market, Fish Market and Red House buildings, as well as the old engine house, at the western end of the site. This aims to bring new investment and active use back to this part of Smithfield, while respecting its heritage. Smithfield remains a key infrastructure hub, with a new Crossrail station at Farringdon and a recent refurbishment of the Holborn Viaduct. Eon is also undertaking a major refurbishment of the existing Combined Heat & Power (CHP) plant at Smithfield to extend its life for another 30 years. Work on this begins in late 2013 and will be substantially complete in early 2015.

Two other significant City's Estate holdings are the Conduit Mead Estate and the Tottenham Court Road Estate. The former, named after the source of the water supply from Tyburn to the City, originally comprised the whole of New Bond Street, Brook Street, Conduit Street, Grafton Street and South Molton Street, and was mostly developed in the 18th century. The properties here consist largely of retail with offices and residential above, some of which is in direct ownership while others are subject to 2000 year leases. A policy of long-term refurbishment and public realm improvement is in place. The Tottenham Court Road Estate, partly in direct ownership, was acquired in 1574 in an exchange of lands with Sir Nicholas Bacon (see also Colville Estate, page 39), who sought ownership of land held by the City in Lincoln's Inn Fields. The City has been reinvesting in properties here over the last decade, including a major commercial refurbishment at the corner of Tottenham Court Road, Store Street and South Crescent.

The income derived from the Bridge House Estates is used to maintain the four road bridges across the Thames – London, Southwark, Blackfriars and Tower Bridge – and also, from 2002, the Millennium Bridge. The surplus funds of £15 million per year are used to assist charitable organisations throughout Greater London via the City Bridge Trust, founded in 1995. The majority of properties in Finsbury Circus, largely developed by the late 19th century, lie within the Bridge House Estates. Here the City is reinvesting in upgrading and refurbishing office and retail, for example 1/5 London Wall Buildings, in recognition that this area, between Moorgate and Liverpool Street, will see significant change with the arrival of Crossrail.

www.cityoflondon.gov.uk

Right: 'New Sights of London' exhibition: architectural model of the Barbican, 1960. Courtesy of the London Metropolitan Archives
Below: London Wall Place, Make Architects
Below right: Tottenham Court Road Estate, 1899. Courtesy of the London Metropolitan Archives

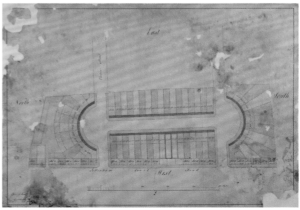

The Duchy of Lancaster

The Duchy of Lancaster was founded in the 13th century as a portfolio of land, property and assets held in trust for the Sovereign in his or her role as Duke of Lancaster (the title remains 'duke' for a female sovereign) – it constitutes private property and so it is not part of The Crown Estate. The main holding in London, held as part of the Duchy since 1284, is the Savoy Estate on the site of the old Savoy Palace and with the 500-year-old Queen's Chapel of The Savoy at its centre (but not the Savoy Hotel). The London portfolio is valued at about £110 million, 69 per cent of the total urban property value; there are also properties in the Midlands and northern England.

It comprises mostly shops and offices and is managed by the Duchy Office under the direction of the Urban Surveyor of Lands, who is responsible for promoting new development opportunities on Duchy land. These are either developed directly or in partnership. Its most recent development project, the £9 million refurbishment of the 1930s Wellington House on the corner of the Strand and Lancaster Place, is part of a long-term programme to upgrade the Savoy Estate properties to retain financial value, while also exploiting a perceived gap in the market for high-quality office accommodation in the Strand and Midtown area. Wellington House was completed in September 2012 and provides 40,000 sq ft of flexible office space and a new top floor with views over the Thames.

The Savoy Estate sold three long leaseholds: Brettenham House to Drace in 2007, 111 Strand to Rushmere Properties in 2000 and Savoy Hill House to the Institute of Electrical Engineers in 1997. It also owns the freehold of 1 Lancaster Place and 9 Savoy Street, a 23,500 sq ft scheme that houses the Duchy's headquarters and other office tenants, and the 42,000 sq ft Norman House comprising office and retail.

The Duchy of Lancaster has also joined the partnership to set up the Northbank Business Improvement District with occupiers Coutts, PWC and the Savoy and Corinthia hotels, among others. The BID aims to address issues such as encouraging more footfall to the area, such as tourists who visit theatres in Covent Garden and those leaving Charing Cross station en route to Leicester Square, providing better infrastructure and pavements for cyclists and pedestrians, and improving the Strand's retail offer.

www.duchyoflancaster.co.uk

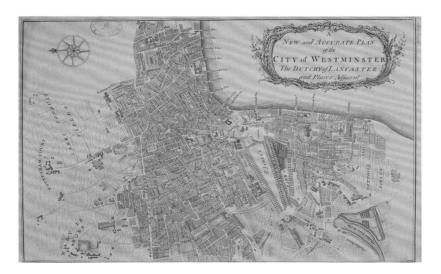

Right: Plan of the City of Westminster, The Duchy of Lancaster and the adjacent area, c.1760. Courtesy of the London Metropolitan Archives

The Duchy of Cornwall

The Duchy of Cornwall is a private estate invested in the eldest son of the sovereign (or, if there is no son, dormant in the Crown). It was created in 1337 by Edward III to provide his heir apparent, the Black Prince, with an independent source of income. The Duchy owns 53,154 hectares of land across 24 counties, principally a combination of farms, small holdings, residential properties, shops and offices, with a total net capital value in 2011/12 of £728 million. Following an Act of Parliament in 1863, the Duchy is run by the Prince's Council, a non-executive board chaired by the Prince of Wales (the Duke of Cornwall).

In London the Manor of Kennington formed part of the original grant of 1337, and comprises both residential and commercial properties. Large-scale residential development took place in the 19th century with urban growth in south London resulting from the building of Vauxhall Bridge in 1812 and Waterloo Bridge in 1817. These included the Vauxhall Model Lodging Houses (1854), tenement flats on Sancroft Street and Chester Way, and in the early 20th century substantial development of Kennington, beginning with the cottages in Denny Street, and followed by the construction of Courtenay Square and Cardigan Street. Most of the residential estate was sold to London & Quadrant in July 1990. Approximately 50 flats and houses remain within the Duchy's portfolio and these are intended to be retained, through a programme of refurbishment and reletting. The Crown Estate has reportedly also sold some residential stock at the Oval to the Duchy of Cornwall.

The commercial portfolio, valued at £75 million, is based on historic assets ranging from office premises to the Oval Cricket Ground. A major programme to upgrade the latter began in 2004 with the OCS stand designed by HOK Sport (Populous) completed in 2005. A second phase involved refurbishing and extending the historic Members' Pavilion, built in 1892, to give the ground a new front of house facade towards Oval station.

www.duchyofcornwall.org

Right: 2-20 Newburn Street, front elevations, 1957. Courtesy of the London Metropolitan Archives

The Mercers' Company

The Mercers' Company, which received its first royal charter in 1394, is the largest of the City livery companies and the first in the order of precedence. Mercers derives from the word 'mercery' and originally comes from the Latin term 'merx' which means merchandise. In England it came to refer specifically to trade in luxury fabrics, and so mercers were originally London merchants who dealt in the import and export of textiles from abroad. The Company grew significantly in the intervening years but during the sixteenth century its connection to and membership engagement with the original trade diminished.

Today the Company is a predominantly philanthropic organisation and associated with several charitable trusts and responsible for a significant grants programme that supports education, general welfare, church and faith, and arts and heritage. These activities are funded by income derived from its investments, principally the extensive property portfolio. In addition, The Mercers' Company retains responsibility for managing several almshouses and other homes for the elderly (associated with the charitable trusts the company oversees) as well as the running of 17 schools across the UK.

The Company estates are a combination of properties owned by different charitable trusts for which the Company is trustee and those that have been acquired to grow the portfolio.

The Charity of Sir Richard Whittington, the former Lord Mayor of London (and Master of the Company), established a college of priests and an almshouse (Whittington College), which is now based in Surrey. This constitutes some of the earliest properties bequeathed to the Company. It still includes properties let on long leases in the City including in Gresham Street, King's Arms Yard and Moorgate. The Colet Estate was an endowment by John Colet, Dean of St Paul's Cathedral and a member of the Company, used to found St Paul's School in 1509. The estate derived from property in Buckinghamshire and Stepney, but all of the property in the latter

Below: Portrait of Sir Thomas Gresham, aged 24, artist unknown, 1544. Courtesy of the Mercers' Company © Louis Sinclair
Right: South front of second Royal Exchange, Robert White, 1671

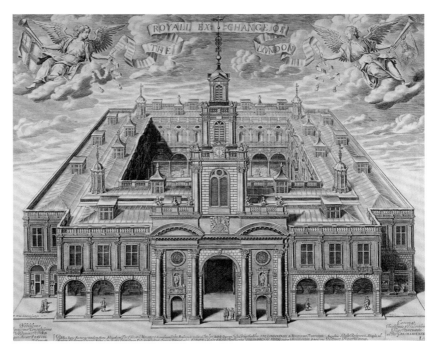

has been sold, primarily as part of a compulsory purchase by the Greater London Council in the 1960s.

The Company's principal estates today are in the City and in Covent Garden. The City properties include Mercers' Hall, the third in its history after earlier incarnations were destroyed (in the Great Fire of 1666 and the Blitz), and the Royal Exchange. Founded by Sir Thomas Gresham in the 16th century, the Royal Exchange was bequeathed by him alongside other properties, jointly to The Mercers' and The City of London Corporation. Since 1597 the Gresham Estate has been managed by a committee called the Joint Grand Gresham Committee, comprising representatives of both The Mercers' and the City, in line with Sir Thomas' original bequest. The Royal Exchange has twice during its history been destroyed by fire. It was substantially redeveloped in 2001 to house luxury boutique shops, a courtyard bar and restaurant, as well as extensive office space.

The Mercers' Covent Garden portfolio, which represents the majority part of its holdings, consists of six blocks of property on the north side of Long Acre. It was left to the Company in 1530 on the death of Lady Joan Bradbury, who had acquired approximately 149 acres of agricultural land in the parishes of Marylebone, St Giles and St Martin in the Fields to endow a chantry. The bequest was reduced in size by Henry VIII in 1542. Today the 8-acre area, which underwent extensive regeneration and renovation, includes shops, cultural spaces, offices and flats.

For the Company, stewardship of its assets, not least the safeguarding and development of the property portfolio, is vital to continuing the charitable and educational support it provides. During the past decade the Company has almost doubled the size of its freehold estate in the City, with the majority subject to long leasehold interests. In Covent Garden the entire estate is freehold, generally subject only to direct occupational interests. As these interests have expired the properties have been subject to an ongoing programme of refurbishment and upgrading. Residential units are let on Assured Shorthold Tenancies only. In 2012 the Company also entered into an agreement with the Donmar Warehouse to redevelop its properties at 1-5 Dryden Street and 4-6 Arne Street. The former will become the Donmar Dryden Street, designed by Haworth Tompkins, and leased to the theatre, and will provide a rehearsal space, offices, education space and residence for visiting artists. The latter will be converted into commercial and residential use and let by the Company on short leases.

To secure and grow the benefits to its Covent Garden estate, The Mercers' Company has entered into a joint venture, Longmartin, with its neighbouring land owner, Shaftesbury PLC (see page 96). The objective is to revitalise that end of Long Acre to ensure Covent Garden retains its identity as one of London's key visitor and retail hubs. St Martin's Courtyard was completed in 2011, and features 25 shops, eight restaurants, 10,000 sqm offices and 75 flats between Long Acre, Shelton Street and Mercer Street, centred on a new public space. The retail offer, which encompasses contemporary boutiques and international flagship stores, complements the more mainstream offering of the Covent Garden piazza,. The scheme was designed in phases by Smith Caradoc-Hodgkins Architects and the MR Partnership, which acted as strategic architects.

The Mercers' Company's next project, due for completion in 2015 subject to planning consent, is Mercers' Yard, designed by Ian Ritchie Architects. This is a proposed mixed-use residential development, composed of three new warehouse-proportioned buildings characteristic of the area and an existing and enhanced warehouse, creating new interconnecting public spaces edged with shops.

Above: Study view towards the Mercers' Yard development proposed piazza © Ian Ritchie Architects Ltd
Right: The Royal Exchange, 2012. Courtesy of the Mercers' Company © Louis Sinclair

www.mercers.co.uk

JUBILEE WALKWAY

The Eton College Estate

The Eton College Estate traces its origins to 1440, when Henry VI granted the Manor of Chalcots, an area around what is now Chalk Farm, to the now famous school that he had founded in Berkshire. For centuries it remained agricultural land cultivated by tenant farmers, but its potential for development was first recognised in 1796 when the then college surveyors advised "a considerable part of this estate is eligibly situated for building" because of the roads from London north (now Haverstock Hill and Finchley Road).

Encouraged by the building boom to the south, around Regent's Park, the College granted building leases in the 1840s to Samuel Cuming, who constructed stuccoed pairs of villas, with Italian style eaves, along Adelaide Road, Provost Road and Eton Road (now a conservation area). St Saviour's Church was built in 1850. These houses, in a modest-sized development, were intended for less affluent professional workers. Villa development continued in the later 19th century but the area was substantially redeveloped in the 20th, with the central 35 acres being replanned as the Chalcots Estate by the London Borough of Camden.

Below: Harley Road, c1905. Courtesy of English Heritage

Founded: 1444

The Leathersellers' Company

Like The Mercers' Company, The Leathersellers' Company is one of London's historic City livery companies and received its royal charter in 1444 to regulate the sale of leather within the City of London. It is now provides charitable grants and support for education and the British leather trade. In the mid-15th century a group of trustees acting for the Company purchased five tenements on the south side of London Wall near Moorgate, part of which the Leathersellers used as their livery hall.

In the 16th century the Company grew wealthier through bequests of money, plate and property, and, seeking to build a larger hall, it bought the former priory of St Helen's, Bishopsgate, in 1543 and converted it. This hall was demolished in 1799 and the company moved to a nearby site; in order to improve its income its entire City estate was cleared, and John Nash was commissioned to draw up plans for a grand square.

The Company, however, eventually chose an unknown pair of local developers who began work in 1802 on a cul-de-sac of houses which became the first St Helen's Place, rents from which supported the rising wealth of the Company in the 19th century. The livery hall was rebuilt on different sites several times in the 19th and 20th centuries; the sixth hall, at St Helen's Place, opened in 1960 and was occupied by the company until early 2011.

The Leathersellers' Company is the freeholder of 100 Bishopsgate, a new landmark tower in the City of London being developed jointly by Brookfield Properties and Great Portland Estates and let on a long lease. Also included in the scheme will be the redeveloped 5-7 St Helens Place, housing a new livery hall for the Company, which will retain full control of the site. The scheme will retain the original façade and Eric Parry Architects has been appointed to fit out the Hall shell, which is expected to complete in 2016.

www.leathersellers.co.uk

Right: St Helen's Place

Founded: 1553

The Skinners Company (Tonbridge School Estate)

As in the case of most City livery companies, the London properties owned by the Worshipful Company of Skinners – which controlled the English fur trade until the 18th century – were bequeathed by members of the company as endowments for educational and charitable purposes. The main estate owned by the Company is the Sandhills or Tonbridge School Estate in St Pancras, covering an area to the north and south of what is now the Euston Road. Sir Andrew Judd, a leading member of the company, left this land (and land in Gracechurch Street in the City) as an endowment for Tonbridge School, which he founded in 1553. The income from these estates remains at the disposal of the Governors of the school for its general benefit.

Residential building began on the estate before 1799, but the southern part remained mainly farmland until 1807, until the Company was effectively forced into development by the encroaching Foundling Estate to the south. In the 20th century the Estate sold the freeholds of much of its Bloomsbury property, and its Burton Street and Bidborough Street residential properties were let on long leases to the London Borough of Camden, and others in Cartwright Gardens to London University and private hotels.

The Company also owned the area known as Clarke's Close in Clerkenwell, bequeathed to it by John Meredith, a Master of the Company, in 1633 for charitable purposes. In the early 19th century it leased the land to James Whiskin, who built Skinners Street and Whiskin and Meredith Streets, residential streets that were occupied largely by Clerkenwell tradesmen.

Below: Courtyard of the Grade I listed Skinner's Hall, home to the Skinners for over 700 years

www.skinnershall.co.uk

Founded: 1554
[land leased in 1532]

The Portman Estate

The Portman Estate, covering 110 acres in Marylebone, dates back to the 16th century, when Sir William Portman, Lord Chief Justice to Henry VIII, originally from Orchard Portman in Somerset, leased 270 acres of the Manor of Lileston (Lisson). He acquired the freehold in 1554, but most of the land remained farmland and meadow until the mid-18th century and the building boom after the end of the Seven Years' War in 1763.

In the 1750s William Baker had leased land from the family to lay out Orchard and Portman Streets, and the north side of Oxford Street. Henry William Portman, a descendant of Sir William, continued the development in 1764 with the creation of Portman Square, with buildings by James Wyatt, Robert Adam and James 'Athenian' Stuart, including Montagu House, built in the north-west corner for the famed literary hostess Elizabeth Montagu and later used by the Portman family as their London town house.

Portman Square was the focus of the new estate and was followed by the building of Manchester Square during the 1770s and Bryanston and Montagu Squares 30 years later. These were laid out by the Estate's architect, James Thompson Parkinson. The area remained largely residential, attracting the prosperous middle class who wanted to live near the city centre. There were also mews for tradesmen and servants. At the southwest corner of the Estate, where Marble Arch now stands, were the Tyburn gallows, London's principal place of public execution until 1783.

Development of the area north of the Marylebone Road around Dorset Square continued after 1815, and to the north west in Lisson Green, workers' cottages were

Right: Estate boundaries, 1888.
Photograph: Sabera Bham

033

built from 1820 to 1840. Many of the original Georgian houses north of Portman Square were redeveloped as mansion blocks, which were let on long leases. This development spread along the major traffic routes of Edgware Road and Baker Street.

In 1948 the Estate, then valued at £10 million, was subject to death duties of £7.6 million on the death of the seventh Viscount Portman, resulting in the sale of all the family's West Country estates as well as the northern part of the London Estate in 1951, and the area around Crawford Street the following year. In the later 1950s and 1960s the Estate collaborated with the developer Max Rayne to redevelop the frontage of Oxford Street and Baker Street, as well as the south and west sides of Portman Square.

The London Estate today covers the area from Edgware Road in the west to beyond Baker Street in the east, and north almost as far as Crawford Street. Unlike many other estates, The Portman Estate has a distinctive multicultural aspect, with its Middle Eastern community established in and around Edgware Road since the 1970s. The typology of the Estate is divided equally between residential, commercial and retail in order to ensure a robust and diverse portfolio. The Portman Estate is owned by a series of family trusts, and has invested considerably in refurbishment and upgrading properties to maintain the quality of stock, with a continuing investment programme of £140 million over the next five years.

The residential portfolio, 50 per cent of which is Grade II listed, is a combination of distinctive Georgian classical town houses and redbrick mansion flats. Overall 625 flats are directly controlled, and most units rented on short term agreements. Investment had been focused on continually upgrading stock, including structural works and the reinstatement of historic features, to create high-end

Below: 10 Portman Square, designed by Jestico + Whiles

Above: 52 Gloucester Place, refurbished by Feilden+Mawson

residential properties. Such work has taken place in Gloucester Place, for example, where 27 properties have recently been completely refurbished. Alongside this the Estate has sought to enhance its high-quality customer service and facilities management provision.

The Estate has more than 130 retail units in direct control, centred primarily on Portman Village – Seymour Place and New Quebec Street – and on Chiltern Street. In the former, it has built on the heritage of these areas as local high streets to create a retail destination for fashion, restaurants and independent boutiques, including coffee houses and perfumeries, reinforced by the Portman Village brand concept promoted through a bespoke website, benefits scheme for shoppers and visitors, and events such as an annual summer street party. A similar strategy is being employed at Chiltern Street, where all 49 units reverted on the expiry of the headlease in 2009. The street is an increasingly well recognised retail destination, and its status will be further enhanced by improved parking and pavements, as well as the completion of a discrete luxury five star boutique hotel in the Grade II listed Old Fire Station, at the end of 2013.

To expand its Grade A office stock, while also creating a signpost to Portman Village, the Estate has entered a joint venture with British Land to replace the Victorian Marble Arch House at the junction of Edgware Road and Seymour Street with a substantial mixed-use development. The scheme (due to complete in autumn 2013) comprises 60,000 sq ft of offices and 31,000 sq ft of retail and residential accommodation. It aims to deliver a BREEAM Excellent rating through the use of passive design strategies supplemented by low-energy mechanical systems and a solar thermal array providing hot water for the adjacent residential block. The residential accommodation is provided in a reconstructed and extended Victorian block, which aims to achieve Level 3 under the Code for Sustainable Homes. The Estate is keen to improve its environmental position, with all refurbishments aiming to enhance their EPC rating to the minimum of a 'D' – not easy with so many listed Georgian buildings – achieving at least a 'C' in the vast majority of cases.

Another key area of importance for the Estate is the Baker Street Quarter, a new Business Improvement District (BID) established in April 2013 and of which the Estate is a partner. The BID encompasses areas around Portman Square and Manchester Square as well as the length of Baker Street from Marylebone Road in the north to Wigmore Street and down to Orchard Street in the south. It aims to create a high-quality public realm, develop a new brand, identity and public programme to support businesses in the area, and to develop a prime location for corporate business activity in the West End.

Like many estates, The Portman Estate also takes Corporate Social Responsibility seriously, viewing it as an integral part of its business activity. The Estate's community work has resulted in support to the formation of the Edgware Road Partnership (as well as the Baker Street BID), and improvements to the public realm in Portman Square and Chiltern Street. In addition, the Estate has overseen the planting of over 40 trees across its London estate. It also continues to support Westminster Charities – for example, Home Start and St Mary's, as well as schools such as Hampden Gurney and sponsorship of the Teach First initiative. Moreover, it regularly reviews a schedule of residential tenants who may be vulnerable for health, age or financial reasons. In 2013, The Portman Estate won the Westminster City Council and the Volunteer Centre in Westminster's Partnership Award for their work with St John's Hospice.

www.portmanestate.co.uk

The Harpur Trust (Bedford Charity)

The Bedford Charity (now known as the Harpur Trust) was established in 1566 by Sir William Harpur, who had become Lord Mayor of London in 1561, for the benefit of a grammar school (now Bedford School) he had already helped to found with his wife, Alice, in his home town of Bedford. The endowment originally consisted of the schoolhouse (now the Old Town Hall) and some property in Bedford, and 13 and a half acres of farmland in Holborn.

The latter encompassed an area south of the Rugby estate and north and east of Red Lion Square, including the southern half of what is now Lamb's Conduit Street. It was developed residentially from about 1686, largely by Nicholas Barbon, and much earlier than other estates because of its closeness to Gray's Inn and areas to the south and east of what is now Bloomsbury that already had been developed. In 2011/12 the value of the London estate, now managed by Farebrother, was more than £45.5 million.

As well as supporting the grammar school, Harpur's endowment also made provision for the award of dowries on the marriage of 'poor maids' of the town, for poor children to be 'nourished and informed', and for any remaining income to be distributed amongst the poor. Over the centuries the charity has evolved and its objectives are now the promotion of education; the relief of those who are sick or in need, hardship or distress; and the provision of recreational facilities with a social welfare purpose. Endowments from both the London and Bedford properties support Bedford Academy and other maintained schools and grant funds for individuals and organisations in Bedford in line with the stated objectives. In 2012 the Bedford Charity formerly rebranded as The Harpur Trust and became an incorporated company limited by guarantee.

www.harpurtrust.org.uk

Below: Harpur Street.
Photograph: Agnese Sanvito

The Rugby School Estate

Income from property held in central London has helped to support Rugby School in Warwickshire since its foundation in 1567 by a bequest made by Lawrence Sherriff or Sherriffe, a Rugby-born London grocer and purveyor of spices to Elizabeth I. His bequest included an 8-acre pasture in Conduit Close, which at the time could not be built on as it was outside the London city walls where development was not then permitted.

Residential development began in the early 18th century, as the City spread north and west to reach it, and its income grew rapidly. Some 149 houses and the chapel on Chapel Street were recorded in 1814. Its popularity as a residential area declined from the 1820s – parts later became slums – and in the 20th century land was sold to the Great Ormond Street Hospital. In 1974 the estate sold 42 freeholds to Camden Borough Council.

Today the core of the remaining Rugby Estate, which is now managed by Farebrother, is in the northern end of Lamb's Conduit Street, and parts of Rugby Street, Orde Hall Street and Great Ormond Street. The school retains the freehold to more than 20 shops, 18,000 sq ft of offices and 112 homes in the area. Lamb's Conduit Street's profile as a quirky, local shopping street has been the focus of recent activity: the street has attracted independent retailers, including small fashion, accessories, interiors and homeware shops, as well as booksellers and galleries.

The school's financial statement in 2011 shows a balance of £39.8 million for its London estate. After the costs of its maintenance and administration, 20 per cent of the income is paid to Rugby's neighbouring state school, the Lawrence Sheriff School. The remainder funds Rugby School's long-term capital projects, and foundations and scholarships.

Right: Lamb's Conduit Street.
Photograph: Agnese Sanvito

Founded: 1578

The John Lyon Estate

John Lyon, a yeoman farmer from Harrow, was granted a Royal Charter by Elizabeth I in 1572 to found a free grammar school for boys, which became Harrow School. The Charter anticipated that John Lyon would establish a separate trust for the purpose of maintaining two Roads from London to Harrow, now the Edgware and Harrow Roads. In 1578 John Lyon provided an endowment in the form of a farm of some 48 acres in the area now known as Maida Vale for that purpose, with the first building appearing in 1819, and the wide avenue of Hamilton Terrace created during the 1820s.

Several hundred years later the income from the Maida Vale estate continued to be paid to the authorities responsible for the Roads. In 1991 a Charity Commission scheme came into effect giving the Governors of Harrow School discretion to apply the income for the benefit of the inhabitants of the nine London boroughs served by the two Roads. Now, the Charity is one of the largest grant-givers in London, awarding over £65 million in grants since 1991. One-third of the Charity's income is derived directly from the estate, the remaining two-thirds from the reinvestment of the proceeds of the estate over the last 200 years.

www.johnlyonscharity.org.uk

Right: Close up of the Marylebone map of 1834, showing the estate's holdings along Edgware Road and the beginnings of the layout of Hamilton Terrace

The Colville Estate

The Colville Estate Limited is a privately owned company, with some 100 shareholders, almost all of whom are direct descendants of Sir Nicholas Bacon (1510–1579), Lord Keeper of the Seal during the reign of Queen Elizabeth I and father of the philosopher and statesman Sir Francis Bacon.

The company owns the freehold of a number of commercial properties in the Chancery Lane area, which have been in the ownership of the Bacon family for over 400 years. Last year Colville granted a new 128-year head lease to Derwent London on one of its properties and Derwent are currently engaged in creating a new 100,000 sq ft development on the site. Colville will retain an interest in the rental from the new building.

In recent years the company has been instrumental in setting up the Chancery Lane Association Limited to represent the interests of landowners and occupiers in the Chancery Lane area, with a view to enhancing the appearance and reputation of the street and the immediate surrounding area.

Below: 40 Chancery Lane, Bennetts Associates Architects

Founded: 1609–10

The Marquess of Salisbury's Estate

The Marquesses of Salisbury are descendants of William Cecil, Baron Burghley, Elizabeth I's chief minister. The family originally acquired property around the Strand during the late 16th and early 17th centuries, though none of this now belongs to them. In 1609–10 Robert Cecil, Earl of Salisbury, acquired part of St Martin's Field and began developing the west side of St Martin's Lane, up to Leicester Square. Castle Street, Bear Street, Cranbourn Alley, Cranbourn Passage and Cranbourn Street were all laid out from the 1620s.

The family's property holdings in this area were much reduced in the 19th century, although some residential and commercial properties were retained: in 1843 the second Marquess of Salisbury sold land on the west side of Upper St Martin's Lane and the south side of Cranbourn Street to the Commissioners of Woods and Forests for the widening of both streets and the eastward extension of Cranbourn Street, then famous for its milliners' shops. Later, the third Marquess sold ground on the west side of Castle Street to the Metropolitan Board of Works for the laying out of Charing Cross Road.

Founded: 1619

The Dulwich Estate

The Dulwich Estate comprises property owned by a registered charity that was originally established by Edward Alleyn, the founder of Dulwich College, in 1619. An actor who had made money controlling licences as 'Master of the Royal Game of Bears, Bulls and Mastiffs', he bought the manor of Dulwich and decided to create a charitable foundation and school for poor boys, endowing it with his estate and other property.

In the 19th century increased land values and the building of the railways on endowment lands provided income for the extensive rebuilding of the College to the design of Charles Barry, and to support two other schools, Alleyn's School and James Allen Girls' School, as well as Christ's Chapel (built in 1616) and, until 1995, Dulwich Picture Gallery. In 1882 the separate boards of Estate Governors, responsible for managing the Estate, and College Governors, responsible for the schools, chapel and gallery, were established.

The reconstruction of the Crystal Palace in Norwood in 1854 and the extension of the railway led to extensive residential development on the Estate, including large villas in the mid-19th century, although a rigorous policy of conservation enabled the retention of extensive areas of green space, including Dulwich Park, giving the estate almost a village atmosphere. Today, residential and commercial property is still leased to generate income for the charity and the school (the Board of Estates Governors was reconstituted as the Trustees of the Dulwich Estate in 1995).

There are 5,000 residential properties – houses, flats and maisonettes – on 1,500 acres. Most owners have acquired the freehold interest with the arrival of leasehold reform, but there is a scheme of management in place requiring them to obtain consent for alterations and ensure their properties are well-maintained. The terms of the enfranchisement also requires freeholders to pay a service charge to cover the cost of repairs, maintenance and other works to common areas. Approximately 600 flats and maisonettes are leasehold, with the Estate retaining the freehold. It also owns commercial properties in Dulwich Village, including shops, restaurants, and pubs.

www.dulwichestate.co.uk

Above: Red brick of the
Dulwich Estate

Founded: 1628

The Wellcome Trust Estate (formerly The Smith Charity Estate)

The Smith Charity Estate was founded by Henry Smith, a Tudor salt merchant and successful businessman who created several charitable trusts for the relief of the poor and acquired land across England during his lifetime. The £2,000 left in his will after his death in 1628 was the basic endowment of the original Henry Smith (Kensington Estate) Charity (originally for 'the poorest of my kindred' and 'the relief and ransom of poor captives being slaves under Barbary pirates'). The Trustees of the Charity bought land in the parishes of Kensington, Chelsea and St Margaret's Westminster, most of the income being generated from 70 acres. Today the Charity remains a grantmaking organisation providing a total of up to £25 million each year to up to 1,000 organisations and charities throughout the UK that work to reduce social inequality and economic disadvantage.

In the 17th century most of the estate land in Kensington was covered by nurseries and market gardens, but it was developed from the late 18th throughout to the 20th centuries with elegant terraces, crescents and squares designed by George Basevi and Charles James Freake in a predominantly Italianate style. Many of the streets, such as Onslow Square, Egerton Crescent, Sydney Place and Sumner Place, were named after the Charity's Trustees.

In 1995 54 acres and 2,300 properties – one of the largest residential estates in London – were sold to the Wellcome Trust, a global charitable foundation supporting biomedical research and the medical humanities, in a move by the Smiths Charity to reduce its high exposure to property in its portfolio of assets. The estate now forms the Trust's major property asset and generates income to support its extensive research grants programme.

www.wellcome.ac.uk

Below: Pelham Crescent

Founded: 1660

Trinity Village (formerly The Newington (Trust) Estate)

Trinity Village – centred on Trinity Church Square and Merrick Square in Borough – is owned by the Corporation of Trinity House's Maritime Charity, and income from rents on it supports the charity's wider objectives such as almshouses and pensions, cadet training, marine safety, and education. The Corporation acquired what was previously known as The Newington (Trust) Estate in Borough in 1660 on condition that it was held in trust for charitable purposes.

Along with the two squares, the estate consists of substantial parts of Trinity Street, Cole Street, Swan Street and Falmouth Road, and most of it was made a conservation area in 1968. Trinity Church Square was built between 1824 and 1832 by William Chadwick. Although originally constructed as individual houses, much of the square has been converted laterally into flats across two or three house widths. There are a total of 60 houses on the estate together with some 365 flats. All new tenancies are Assured Shorthold Tenancies. Some freeholds have been sold.

With a requirement to secure a steady and increasing rental income, Trinity House appointed NB Real Estate (now Capita Symonds) to manage the estate in 2005. The estate was rebranded as Trinity Village. The aim was to make Trinity Village a location of choice for residential renters in SE1, and as such improvements to the fabric of the buildings have been made as well as a programme of refurbishment of individual premises pursued. New development opportunities have also been identified, with five units on Swan Street and seven units on Cole Street completed in 2012. Trinity Village has achieved steady growth in rental income in recent years in line with the market.

www.trinityvillage.co.uk

Below: Trinity Church Square

Founded: 1662

The Pollen Estate

The Pollen Estate covers a compact but substantial area of Mayfair largely bounded by Conduit Street, Burlington Gardens, New Bond Street and Regent Street. Comprising the freehold of more than 40 properties, it is now managed by Deloitte Real Estate, and encompasses the highest-value retailing street in the UK (New Bond Street). It now includes predominantly office and retail accommodation.

In 1812 the Reverend George Pollen left the property to Trustees in trust for his five daughters, and the estate is currently governed by a 1966 Deed of Family Arrangement (albeit varied in both 2002 & 2011); currently there are 127 'beneficiaries', both individuals (the majority being the original descendants of Rev Pollen) and charities, with The Church Commissioners the largest; each beneficiary owns a defined percentage of each property on the estate. The estate deed stipulates that it can invest only in the locality.

In recent years a retail strategy for Savile Row has been developed which seeks to protect and enhance its international reputation as a centre of excellence for menswear and tailoring; some of the leases in this street are restricted to tailoring use. The Estate works with Westminster City Council and Savile Row Bespoke to protect the street's tailoring heritage, with Alexander McQueen's London flagship store (2012) one of the most significant recent additions, and has recently initiated public realm and parking improvements.

The Estate has also recently received consent to redevelop part of its holdings on Cork Street and New Bond Street to create new office, retail and art gallery spaces behind existing facades, as well as a residential scheme in Maddox Street.

www.thepollenestate.com

Right: New Bond Street

The Bedford Estates

The Bedford Estates today is synonymous with Bloomsbury, where it remains the largest private landowner. Bloomsbury – then agricultural fields – came into the ownership of the Russell family, the Earls and later Dukes of Bedford, in 1669, when Lady Rachel Vaughan, daughter and heiress of the 4th Earl of Southampton, married William Russell, son of the 5th Earl of Bedford. The Russell family also then owned Covent Garden, one of the most important developments in the history of London.

The Earl of Southampton was responsible for the creation of the first London square to be so named, Southampton Square (now Bloomsbury Square), by his letting of plots for residential development to the south of his new mansion, Southampton House, built in 1660. Alongside Covent Garden, it was thus one of the earliest examples of development west of the City of London. Great Russell Street was built to connect Tottenham Court Road with the square and mansion house.

The next major phase of development occurred in the late 18th century, which resulted in the fine Georgian architecture which is so characteristic of the area today – including the laying out of Bedford Square and Gower Street. The 5th Duke demolished Bedford House (the renamed Southampton House), replacing it with the broad avenue of Bedford Place linking Bloomsbury Square and the new Russell Square, and his brother the 6th Duke continued by extending the estate up to and beyond Euston Road with square and terraced streets.

Originally the estate was residential and there were legal restrictions on trade uses – as the area became more attractive for professionals and academics there was some relaxation of these restrictions to allow educational use and, for example, for doctors to set up practices. From the late 19th and early 20th centuries, however, Bloomsbury became synonymous with educational and cultural uses, following the expansion of the British Museum and the University of London. The Bedford Estates was obliged to sell land for these growing institutions after compulsory powers for the sale of private land for educational use were implemented. (The 11th Duke of Bedford had also sold Covent Garden in 1918.)

Today the focus of Bedford Estates is on the regeneration and good stewardship of Bloomsbury, London's university quarter, and on maintaining its reputation as a centre of excellence for higher education. This area is also becoming more significant as a business district with the links to the regenerated King's Cross station to the north and Crossrail on its southern boundary. The Estate today remains geographically compact - it comprises approximately 30 acres (12 ha) bounded by Tottenham Court Road to the west, Euston Road to the north, Southampton Row to the east, and New Oxford Street to the south. There are no single houses – all residential property is flats, which constitute about 25 per cent of the estate's income. Properties are both long-lease and shorthold tenancies – the latter have increased considerably in the last 10 years.

There are approximately 200 buildings on the estate, of which just over 50 per cent are listed, and one of The Bedford Estates' main priorities is refurbishment in order to bring the historic buildings up to date with 21st-century facilities and to remedy any structural wear and tear, as well as preserving their distinctive character for the long term. Many buildings have small floorplates and so a substantial part of the estate's office spaces are occupied by diverse smaller businesses. Continuing the holistic approach which is such a distinctive aspect of the London estates today, public realm improvements have been done on a small (but significant) scale, for example replacing 1960s lamps with those more in keeping with the Georgian buildings.

Recently The Bedford Estates has focused on regenerating Store Street to create

a lively local 'village' high street, which acts as an entry point to Bloomsbury and link westwards to Russell Square and the British Museum. The Estate regained control of the buildings on the south side of Store Street in 2010 after an 80-year lease expired. In 2011 it invested £5 million in upgrading the 14 shops and restaurants at 28-42 Store Street both internally and externally to provide a total of around 25,000 sq ft of retail space, with the aim of encouraging a lively and eclectic mix of smaller, independent retailers including coffee shops, bookshops, florists, and hair and beauty salons, among others. The scheme also involved improvements to paving and public realm.

A key element of the scheme was the £2.5 million revamping of the former Bloomsbury Service Station on the corner of Store Street and Ridgmount Street to maintain and update its 1920s character while providing more than 7,000 sq ft of high-quality office space and an anchor restaurant, let to the Byron restaurant at the end of 2012. The upper level of the building also features an artwork commissioned by The Bedford Estates on a 1920s theme, including a biplane representing the aviator Mary, Duchess of Bedford, who died in 1937 on a solo flight. The office development, spread over three floors (approximately 4,800 sq ft in total), incorporates a partly original period facade and, with solar thermal panels and a green roof, has a BREEAM Excellent rating. The Bedford Estates has also invested in the creation of 'above the shops' apartments on Store Street and converted garages beneath existing flats on Ridgmount Street in order to provide more residential space.

In recent years The Bedford Estates has sought to acquire new property – especially more modern office buildings to balance its portfolio. Its focus in this respect is on Tottenham Court Road, where the property type and mix – electronics retailers and 1960s buildings – represents a stark contrast to the smaller, historic properties to the east. In September 2012 it entered into a joint venture with Exemplar Properties to redevelop One Bedford Avenue fronting onto Tottenham Court Road. The aim, subject to planning consent being gained, is to deliver a mixed-use scheme of 120,000 sq ft of retail, office and residential accommodation to be completed in 2016.

www.bedfordestates.com

Left: Plan of intended improvement to the estate, 1800
Above: Store Street redevelopment.
Photograph: John Freeman
Below: Store Street redevelopment, Nick Kane and Garnett+Partners

The Grosvenor Estate

The Grosvenor Estate, owned by Trustees for the benefit of the Grosvenor family, includes all the family's assets but by far and away the best known of these is the London estate which for over 300 years has been centred on Westminster. Today, in addition to the UK business which manages the London estate, The Grosvenor Estate includes; property company Grosvenor Group which has offices in 17 cities around the world and an international fund management business; the Wheatsheaf Group which invests in agribusiness and renewable energy; and a family investment office which manages the other Trust owned assets including rural estates. The Grosvenor family, headed by the Duke of Westminster – a title bestowed on the head of the family in 1874 by Queen Victoria and passed to male heirs – has owned the 300 acres of Mayfair and Belgravia since 1677, when the Cheshire baronet Sir Thomas Grosvenor married Mary Davies, heiress to the Manor of Ebury.

The northern part of the Manor, today bounded by Oxford Street, Park Lane, Berkeley Square and Avery Row, took its name from the May Fair – a 'place of vice and impurities' held annually until the 19th century. The southern part, bounded by Chelsea, Hyde Park, Buckingham Palace and the River Thames, known then as the Five Fields and now as Belgravia and Pimlico, was a mixture of swamp, pasture, orchards and a few scattered houses – and reportedly a haunt of highwaymen and duellists.

Building in Mayfair did not begin until 1720 when Sir Richard Grosvenor appointed Thomas Barlow, the Estate Surveyor, to plan a grid of wide, straight streets with Grosvenor Square (the largest square in London after Lincoln's Inn and larger than Trafalgar Square) at the centre, surrounded by mansions. This plan, of what is one of the most prestigious residential areas in London, remains largely unchanged today despite much rebuilding in the 19th and early 20th centuries.

A century later Robert Grosvenor, 1st Marquess of Westminster, through the Thomas Cundy dynasty of Estate Surveyors (I, II and III), oversaw the development of Belgravia, appointing Thomas Cubitt and Thomas Cundy to develop the area into the classic Regency style of squares, streets and crescents, faced with stucco. One of the keys to the success of Belgravia was Cubitt's exceptional standards in land

Below: Robert Grosvenor, 1st Marquess of Westminster
Below right: Grosvenor Square, 17th century
Far right: Brown Hart Gardens, BDP

A View of Grosvenor Square London | Vue de la Place de Grosvenor a Londres

drainage, sewerage, planting and paving as much as that of building construction. The majority of Pimlico, also developed by Cubitt from the 1830s, remained in the family ownership until it was sold in 1953.

Today the estate is managed from Grosvenor's head office which moved from its original home in Davies Street to Grosvenor Street in 2000. The London estate now consists of a mix of freehold residential, residential and office properties in Mayfair and Belgravia and the overall long-term strategy is to ensure that these areas are managed and maintained as high-quality places in which to live, work and visit. Building on Cubitt's heritage, Grosvenor has been one of the key innovators in understanding the value of investment in public realm and has worked in partnership with Westminster City Council to improve key streets across the estate, drawing on the best practice of international cities such as Copenhagen and Melbourne.

The first phase, for Mount Street in Mayfair and Elizabeth Street in Belgravia, was completed in 2011 and involved removing the 'clutter' of signage, upgrading pavements and introducing pedestrian-only areas as well as public art and other features, including a new water feature by the Japanese architect Tadao Ando for Mount Street. Located just off Berkeley Square, Mount Street has now become established as a luxury retail location in the UK, with high-end cafes and fashion names such as Marc Jacobs, Balenciaga, Christian Louboutin and Lanvin. Subsequent phases have included North Audley Street, Duke Street and the Grade II listed Brown Hart Gardens, which completed earlier this year.

In conjunction with these public realm improvements, Grosvenor is also developing a programme of community-focused events such as street parties and summer activities in Grosvenor Square and Elizabeth Street, to help engender a sense of 'neighbourhood' for both local residents and visitors, especially in Mayfair.

Above: Belgrave Square
Left: Elizabeth Street, BDP

Together with the local amenity societies, residents' groups and businesses, Grosvenor has also been instrumental in helping to establish Neighbourhood Forums for Mayfair & Belgravia as provided for under the Localism Act.

The Estate also encompasses active residents' and traders' associations, particularly in Belgravia, and Grosvenor is represented on the Boards of the two local Business Improvement Districts, Victoria and the New West End Company. The residential portfolio in London includes more than 4,000 properties that range from studio flats to luxury town houses, on long leases, short leases of 20 years or less, and rental; 25 per cent of the total is affordable housing units managed by organisations such as Peabody (see page 80).

Grosvenor is an active developer both within and outside the London estate. Current projects underway or due for completion include 33 Davies Street, a joint venture with Stow Capital Partners to provide a 38,000 sq ft office and retail scheme close to Claridges Hotel. Designed by HOK with traditional brick and Portland stone facades, it is targeted at office occupiers from the financial and business services sectors and high-end retailers. Another significant development forming part of Grosvenor's aim to deliver major office space in Mayfair is a 40,000 sq ft office at 18-20 Grosvenor Street. Arranged over six floors, the floor plates will range from 4,000 sq ft to 7,800 sq ft. The scheme also includes two retail units, at 18 Grosvenor Street and 20 Brook's Mews. The target completion date is early 2015.

Grosvenor is an innovator in seeking to improve the environmental performance of its existing portfolio in London, which includes 1,500 listed buildings. In addition to a number of BREEAM Excellent accredited new build commercial buildings, in May 2013 planning consent was granted for conversion of a Grade II listed building in Ebury Street into three high quality apartments. The project will utilise new sustainable technology including: photovoltaic array, solar thermal heating, air source heat pump, grey water recycling, internal insulation, vacuum glazing and phase change materials. This is a pilot scheme that aims to reduce the building's carbon emissions from 29 tonnes per year to six, meeting the Government's 2050 target of an 80 per cent reduction in emissions and achieving a BREEAM Excellent rating. When completed in 2015, the project will be monitored over a two year study to compare its energy efficiency with other projects in Ebury Street, which have been refurbished to Grosvenor's typical specifications.

www.grosvenorestate.com

Founded: 1693

The Capper Mortimer Estate

The Capper Mortimer Estate adjoined The Bedford Estates, in the north-west corner of Bloomsbury, covering an area bounded by Tottenham Court Road, University Street, Pancras (Capper) Street and Gower Street. Its origins lie in the farm and pasture land originally on this site, owned by Christopher Capper, described as a 'great cow keeper', from as early as 1693. The farmhouse known as Capper's Farm lay on the site of part of what is now Heal's department store; it was demolished only in 1917. The area was also known as the Bromfield site, and later as Brickfields. Residential development began in the later 18th century, after the land had passed to Hans Winthrop Mortimer by 1768. He began the development of Mortimer's Market to the west by 1795.

The eastern part, at the end of University (then Carmarthen) Street and north of the part of Gower Street on the Duke of Bedford's land, was auctioned in 1825 for residential development, but acquired as the site for the then new University of London.

Founded: 1694

The Greenwich Hospital Estates

Greenwich Hospital is a unique Crown charity established in the 17th century to provide support to seamen of the Royal Navy and Royal Marines and their families. In 1694 a royal charter of William and Mary established the Royal Hospital for Seamen (latterly known as Greenwich Hospital). It was designed by Sir Christopher Wren, as a home for retired seamen of the Royal Navy, to provide support for seamen's widows and education for their children, and the improvement of navigation. After the Pensioners left in the 1860s, the Royal Naval College used the Hospital's original buildings from 1873 until July 1996.

The Greenwich Hospital has rural investment property in Northumberland and Suffolk, but the core of its estate is the land originally transferred to the first Greenwich Hospital Commissioners after the Royal Charter of 1694. It later acquired the site of much of what is now the commercial centre of Greenwich, including Greenwich Market, as well as residential premises in Park Row, Eastney Street and Crane Street.

The Old Royal Naval College buildings are presently on a 150-year lease to The Greenwich Foundation – a charity established to take responsibility for preserving, finding new uses for, and encouraging public access to the Royal Hospital site – and the ancillary buildings on a similar long term direct to the University of Greenwich. Greenwich Pier is on a long-term lease to the Port of London Authority.

Over the next five to ten years, Greenwich Hospital is implementing a series of strategies to enhance the vibrant creative, retail and residential community in Greenwich. Key principles will include the creation of prime accommodation to attract high-quality restaurateurs and retailers, returning upper floors wherever possible to residential use, conserving the urban village character by protecting and enhancing the built heritage, and improving the external appearance of the retail and residential frontages.

The aim of the strategy is to further develop Greenwich town centre's positioning and to widen its offer as an eclectic retail area through the addition of a select number of well-known and respected shopping and dining brands, while maintaining the mix of high-quality independent retailers that reflect the identity of Greenwich's creative community.

www.grenhosp.org.uk

Right: Aerial photograph, September 2012

Founded: 17th century

The Ilchester Estates (Holland (Park) Estate)

Much of Holland Park and its surrounding area are owned by the Ilchester Estates, whose property portfolio also includes large areas of the West Country, including Chesil Beach. The estate is almost all residential, comprising flats and houses, covering about 20 acres, and derives from the original Holland Estate, established by Sir Walter Cope, James I's Chancellor, in the 17th century. In 1606 he built the Jacobean mansion later known as Holland House; it was bombed in World War II and later converted into a youth hostel after being sold in 1952 to the London County Council.

Cope's estate was inherited by his son-in-law, Henry Rich, later 1st Earl of Holland, and later sold to the Fox family, who became the Barons Holland. Ultimately the estate passed to the Earls of Ilchester, whose descendants still own it today.

A site that had originally been part of the front park of Holland House was acquired from the Estate on a 999-year lease for the then new Commonwealth Institute, designed by Sir Robert Matthew, Johnson-Marshall and Partners, which opened in 1962. In 2007 the Ilchester Estates, through its company Addison Developments, entered into a joint venture with Chelsfield to redevelop the site, which had been vacated in 2002. The former Commonwealth Institute Exhibition Building, which is listed, is now known as the Parabola and from 2015 will be the new home of the Design Museum. The overall scheme, by Rem Koolhaas and Reinier de Graaf of OMA, will also include three high-end residential buildings and two new public piazzas to create a new cultural destination.

Below: Residential scheme and new Design Museum at the former Commonwealth Institute, OMA

www.ie-properties.co.uk

Founded: 17th century

South Kensington Estates

South Kensington Estates was founded as a property management company for the estate now owned by the Anstruther family but built in the 19th century, located in South Kensington. Its portfolio encompasses the South Kensington Estate (historically known as the Thurloe Estate and more recently, the Alexander Estate) and the Brompton Estate, and it manages, invests in and develops more than 400 residential and commercial properties across this part of London. It includes Thurloe Street, Thurloe Place and the lower part of both Cromwell Place and Exhibition Road, as well as the western end of the Brompton Road and the eastern end of Thurloe Place.

The Alexander Estate was named after its 19th-century owners, but has also been known as the Thurloe Estate after John Thurloe, secretary to the council of state during the Protectorate of the 1650s, and spymaster for Oliver Cromwell, who is said to have given Thurloe land in Brompton for services rendered. Through a complex set of inheritances, the estate passed in the early 19th century to John Alexander, a lawyer. At that time it comprised six separate plots of land over some 54 acres, most of which was let to market gardeners.

Alexander began to develop the land in 1826, contracting with the builder James Bonnin to create a residential area of elegant houses on the eastern side of the estate, but he died in 1831. Much of the subsequent development of the estate was undertaken by his son, Henry Browne Alexander, and progressed in three stages. From 1831 until about the mid-1840s, this involved the extension of the estate created by his father by the laying out of Thurloe Square and adjoining streets, designed by George Basevi. It continued from 1857, and again from 1870 until the 1880s, when all the remaining parts of the estate (mostly west of Gloucester Road) were let to various builders.

In 1863–4 the plan to build the Metropolitan and District Railways resulted in the loss of two separate portions of his estate for the building of South Kensington and later Gloucester Road stations; however, as a result Alexander collaborated with the neighbouring land-owners, Lord Kensington and Robert Gunter, in a scheme of 1866 to extend Cromwell Road westwards from Gloucester Road so as to serve as an artery for all three estates. The western part of the estate was sold in the 1950s to meet death duties.

Right: Empire House
Below: Brompton Quarter, Egerton Terrace junction
© CGL Architects & Designers

In 1905 the Alexander Estate was inherited by Sybil, Lady George Campbell, a great niece of John Alexander, who had married the fourth son of the Duke of Argyll. Today the estate remains in family ownership. The estate was originally almost all residential and, with the impact of leasehold reform, it sold off its remaining enfranchiseable freeholds in 2007. In the 21st century the estate has built on its intimate knowledge of the local area in order to re-establish this part of Kensington as a distinctive place. Today it focuses on reinvesting into residential, buying out long leases to gain direct control and upgrading properties. The estate now is 60 per cent residential by value, but the same percentage commercial, primarily retail and restaurants, by income. There is a policy in place of letting to a business only where the founder remains actively involved.

Until relatively recently it was a traditional estate office, with management, refurbishment and investment outsourced. This changed in 2001-2 when the management of the estate was brought in house. The company extended its property portfolio in 2003 when it bought the Brompton Estate – shops, offices and flats in 197-251 Brompton Road, known as the Brompton Quarter – from the Wellcome Trust, again as a part of a drive to create stronger links and an integrated identity for the areas that are still perceived separately as South Kensington, Brompton and Knightsbridge.

Since then the company has restored and upgraded residential and commercial properties, in particular 223-225 Brompton Road in 2005 (the Brompton Quarter Café), 245-249 Brompton Road (Skandium), the redecoration of its original offices in Thurloe Street, and works carried out to 20 Egerton Gardens Mews in collaboration with the Danish Embassy. It was also a key participant in the plans to improve Exhibition Road.

http://ske.org

Below: Brompton Quarter, facing south along the Brompton Road © CGL Architects & Designers

The Howard de Walden Estate

Over the past decade The Howard de Walden Estate has been instrumental in the revitalisation of Marylebone, 92 acres of which it owns, manages and leases. The estate today comprises the southern half of the original Manor of Tyburn, originally a property of the Crown but sold by James I in 1611. By 1708 the village of Marylebone (taking its name from the parish church of St Mary and the nearby Tyburn river – hence St Mary by the Bourne) comprised a few houses with open fields beyond.

That year John Holles, Duke of Newcastle, acquired the estate and in 1711 it passed to his daughter, Henrietta, who in 1713 married Edward Harley, later 2nd Earl of Oxford. The Earl and Countess commissioned John Prince to draw up a plan for the estate in 1719, with Cavendish Square as the focal point and a grid system of streets to the north, east and west. The chapel and market, essential for any 18th-century estate, were designed by James Gibbs.

The pace of development was slowed by the South Sea Bubble financial collapse in 1720, but continued northwards – including Harley Street, Portland Place and Wimpole Street – under the ownership of the Earl and Countess's daughter, Margaret Cavendish Harley, who had married the 2nd Duke of Portland.

Right: Boundaries of the estate in 1789, Thomas Marsh

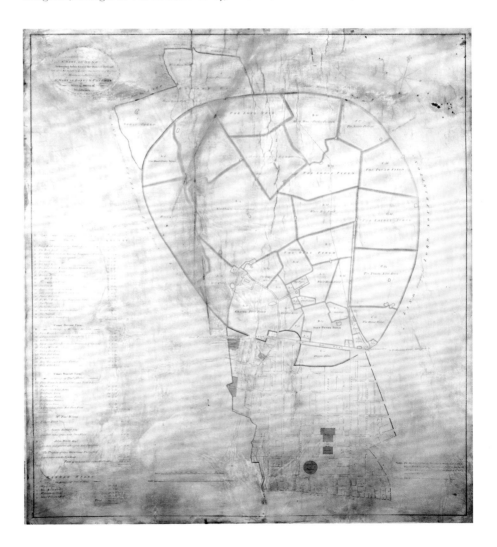

The Portland Estate was renamed The Howard de Walden Estate in 1879 when it passed to the 5th Duke's sister, Lucy, Lady Howard de Walden. Much rebuilding and refurbishment work took place in the 19th century, when the estate, and Harley Street in particular, began to develop its reputation as the leading centre of excellence. The Medical Society of London moved to Chandos Street in 1872 and the Royal Society of Medicine to Wimpole Street in 1912.

In 1914 an area to the north of Marylebone, known as Portland Town, was sold and between the wars a further portion of the estate was sold off to the shipping magnate Sir John Ellerman.

The Howard de Walden Estate is widely recognised for its pioneering and imaginative approach to placemaking. This has been particularly evident in its regeneration of Marylebone High Street as the centre of what is now known as Marylebone Village. In 1995 a third of the shops were either vacant or temporarily occupied; this sparked a change of approach in the Estate, which owned most of the freehold retail, but because of the grant of headleases, actually controlled only about a third of the shops. The new management at the Estate sought to improve the quality and balance of the retail offering by increasing their ownership of the high street to around 70 per cent and by carefully choosing a number of anchor retailers and smaller, independent traders as tenants, with particular emphasis placed on achieving a strong and distinctive mix of retailers.

This regeneration is still continuing. One current focus is on the evolution of Marylebone Lane, a narrow, winding thoroughfare to the north of Oxford Street which follows the route of the River Tyburn. As well as employing its now familiar approach to achieving the right mix of retail and restaurants, the Estate has commissioned the public realm consultancy Publica to formulate proposals to improve the pedestrian environment through changes to pavement lines, resurfacing pavements and roads, and landscaping, with the overall aim of creating better pedestrian connections between Marylebone, Oxford Street and Bond Street, via St Christopher's Place.

The strategic approach taken by the Estate in developing its retail offering is also much in evidence in the three other sectors that make up its core business: medical, office and residential – the latter of which consists of 700 rental properties, varying from studio flats to entire town houses. Central to the Estate's ethos is the belief that for the area to thrive it requires a healthy balance to be maintained between these various sectors, all of which require significant investment. This in turn necessitates an on-going programme of refurbishment and redevelopment in order to ensure that this major conservation area is able to meet the needs of current and future tenants.

The Howard de Walden Estate is home to more hospitals and medical centres than any other estate in London, and medical buildings provide 25 per cent of its income. The majority of the Harley Street Medical Area consists of period town houses which have been converted into medical accommodation for single occupiers or multiple tenants, and these require frequent updating. Drawing heavily upon decades of experience of dealing with listed buildings, the Estate is able to maintain a large portfolio of 18th-century buildings with 21st-century medical facilities.

The Estate has also provided significant investment to create brand new or significantly redeveloped medical buildings, often in partnership with tenants. In 2010 the London Clinic Cancer Centre – a 70,000 sq ft, £80 million joint venture between The Howard de Walden Estate and The London Clinic – became the largest hospital in the private healthcare sector to be built in more than 25 years. In 2013 the Estate leased the 8,000 sq ft 11 Harley Street to Isokinetic, the Italian sports injury clinic, where from 2014 it will provide physiotherapy facilities, including a hydrotherapy pool in the basement of the Grade II-listed building. Other major projects include the refurbishment of 13-18 Devonshire Street as a treatment centre for head and neck cancer run by the private American firm HCA Hospitals, and of 134 Harley Street for the Harley Street Fertility Clinic.

The Estate's commercial buildings have seen a similar blend of refurbishment and redevelopment, with an emphasis on providing office facilities in a broad range of sizes and styles, including plenty of open plan space – a particular challenge given the restrictions imposed by the period building stock. Recent office developments have included the distinctive triangular building at 74 Wigmore Street and the 35,400 sq ft 20 Bentinck Street, which provides highly contemporary facilities behind a retained Edwardian facade.

The Estate's holistic approach to revitalising the area extends well beyond its building works. One of the area's main attractions is its strong sense of community, which the Estate has done much to encourage through its financial support for key local institutions, as well as funding a magazine, several websites and a number of regular community activities. Major events, also largely funded by the Estate, have been put in place to bring vibrancy to the area and provide opportunities for engagement. These include the annual Marylebone Summer Fayre and Marylebone Christmas Lights events, both of which raise money for charity while providing a showcase for local businesses, institutions and retailers.

www.hdwe.co.uk

The Cadogan Estate

In the 16th century the aristocracy and gentry – including Henry VIII's Lord Chancellor, Sir Thomas More – had summer palaces in Chelsea, and the Manor of Chelsea was granted by the King to his last wife, Katherine Parr, in 1543. The Manor was sold to the physician, antiquary and collector Sir Hans Sloane (whose collection formed the core of the British and Natural History Museums) in 1712. In 1717 Charles Cadogan, later 2nd Baron Cadogan, married Elizabeth, Sloane's younger daughter. On Sloane's death in 1753 he left his Chelsea property – which included much of the Manor of Chelsea – to Elizabeth and her heirs. From this The Cadogan Estate in Chelsea originated. Sloane's elder brother also owned property in Chelsea. When he died he left the majority of this to Sir Hans Sloane's other daughter, Sarah Stanley, and from this The Sloane Stanley Estate (see page 64) in western Chelsea is derived.

The development of the Estate did not begin until the 1770s, however, when the architect Henry Holland leased 89 acres of fields from the 1st Earl Cadogan (son of Charles and Elizabeth) between Knightsbridge and the King's Road to build 'Hans Town' – a development of plain brick terraced houses for people of moderate means and what perhaps could be described as the first-ever purpose-built new town. It included the laying out of Sloane Street, Hans Place and Sloane Square, while Holland built his own mansion house, later known as the Pavilion, a grand Palladian-style house on the west side of Sloane Street with 16 acres of meadow and grounds landscaped by his father-in-law, 'Capability' Brown. Only a very few of the Hans Town houses now survive. In 1821 the original lands of the Manor of Chelsea were reconstituted when the Cadogan family inherited the estate of Sarah Stanley.

In the 19th century the Georgian houses built in Chelsea had fallen into decline and many long leases were expiring. This, along with the encroachment of urbanisation (fields had separated Hans Town from Westminster until the development of Belgravia by the Grosvenor Estate) and new transport links with the opening of Sloane Square station encouraged the 5th Earl Cadogan to undertake a major redevelopment of the Estate, under the Cadogan and Hans Place Estate Co., from 1877. Pont Street and Cadogan Square were among the earliest developments in London to feature predominantly red brick rather than stucco.

The modern Cadogan Estate is 50 per cent residential and 50 per cent commercial – and the impact of leasehold enfranchisement has dramatically affected the shape and character of the estate today. The portfolio of leasehold residential has shrunk – 20 years ago the Estate owned the whole of Cadogan, Chelsea and Tedworth Squares, for example – but values have risen. The proceeds of the sale of residential property under the Leasehold Reform Acts have been reinvested into the estate through purchases and development and have included cultural and community projects such as the £1.4 million restoration of Holy Trinity Church and the redevelopment of Cadogan Hall, which is now operated by the Estate as a concert venue.

At the heart of the estate management strategy is a careful curation of the area to maintain long-term vitality and to protect and strengthen Chelsea's international reputation as being one of the world's leading locations in which to live, shop and work. The Estate aims to ensure that what it does in one building benefits the whole street or the wider area, and this principle – that all of the parts contribute to the whole – is instrumental in its approach to taking great care in selecting retail and restaurant tenants particularly. The result is a combination of thriving international brands that have little if any other representation elsewhere in the country, combined with independent stores making up over 40 per cent of the shops.

Recent lettings have included Rag and Bone, a first London store for this New

Below: Pont Street, Cadogan Square
Top right: Beaufort House, Kip's view, 1699
Far right: NEX's competition-winning project for Cadogan Cafe, street elevation

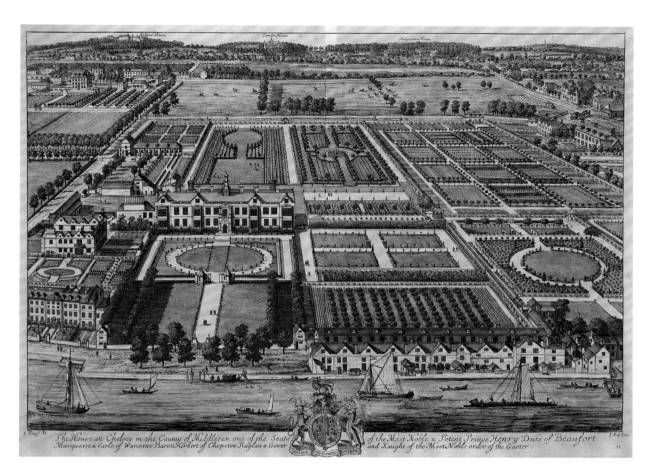

The House att Chelsey in the County of Middlesex one of the Seats of the Most Noble & Potent Prince Henry Duke of Beaufort Marquess & Earle of Worcester Baron Herbert of Chepstow Raglan & Gower and Knight of the Most Noble order of the Garter.

York fashion brand, Tom Ford's sole UK store on Sloane Street, and Massimo Dutti, Gerard Darel from France, the L'Eto Caffe on King's Road, Moyses Stevens Flowers and a plethora of other businesses. Cadogan has established an unusual and innovative lease structure which reflects its close working relationship with incoming retailers and its aim of carefully managing the area. Thus, for example, open market rent reviews have been replaced with annual indexation to better reflect the retailers' businesses, and if the retailer wishes to assign its lease then Cadogan has first right of refusal so that it is able to manage who the new occupier will be.

Cadogan undertakes extensive consumer research to understand who visits the area, where they are from and what attracts them. This research informs retail estate management strategies and shapes consumer marketing of the area. For example, research has highlighted that many people visit the area to meet and hang out with friends as well as to shop. This has resulted in an increased focus on food and beverage.

This is both the result of and a response to the most significant development in the last decade on the estate: the Duke of York's Square, a former barracks on the King's Road transformed by architect Paul Davis & Partners into a mixed-use development of 42 retail units surrounding a major public space. At the heart of the square is a transparent glass pavilion serving as a café, Gelateria Valerie, the success of which has been so overwhelming that the estate initiated a design competition for a new café to replace it, with submissions from leading practices including Architecture 00, Carmody Groarke, and Duggan Morris Architects. In December 2012 NEX was announced as the winner for the £2 million project, which will sit near the entrance to the Saatchi Gallery. The building, in an organic, coiled form, will feature a roof terrace and an ingenious glass wall that will rise and fall depending on the weather.

Cadogan's largest current development is a 135,000 sq ft office and retail scheme at 127-135 Sloane Street, the home of some of the world's most famous designer names including Chloe, Tiffany, Cartier, Pringle and Hugo Boss. The Stiff + Trevillion-designed building at the site of Liscartan House and Granville House involves the demolition of two existing buildings and secured planning consent from the Royal Borough of Kensington and Chelsea at the end of 2011. Works began on site in February 2013 and completion is expected in 2015. The project aims for a BREEAM Excellent rating and will incorporate include photovoltaic cells for the generation of electricity, rainwater harvesting, bicycle storage, planting and green roofs.

A recessed courtyard to the rear, accessed from Pavilion Road, will open onto nine smaller independent retail units and a restaurant, intended to provide a balance with the retail mix on the main thoroughfare of Sloane Street. This reflects the long-term approach to development in providing small shops around a new public environment for visitors to the area to discover and enjoy.

Stewardship has always been at the heart of what Cadogan does, that is, understanding how it can work to support local charities, community projects and the local community as well as actively managing its impact on the environment. It is this holistic approach to managing the estate that led Cadogan to acquire, refurbish and operate Cadogan Hall, which is one of London's leading music venues and home to the Royal Philharmonic Orchestra. This year Cadogan has announced that it will be providing 45 flats at reduced rents for keyworkers. These examples and many more reflect Cadogan's genuine and long-term vested interest in the success of the area.

www.cadogan.co.uk

Date founded: 1716

The Phillimore Estate

The land owned by the Phillimore family in Kensington was once part of the extensive estate attached to Campden House, acquired by Laud D'Oyley in 1708. After his death the following year his son, Robert D'Oyley, sold Campden House and some of its land, leaving 64 acres to the south and west of Campden House, and 20 acres to the north (the latter part was known as The Racks and was sold in 1808). In 1716 Robert bequeathed this estate to his half-sister, Anne, who had married Joseph Phillimore, and her sons.

The area that now comprises The Phillimore Estate was developed by Anne's great-grandson, Charles Phillimore, from 1855. In that year he entered into an agreement with Joseph Gordon Davis to develop 21 acres bounded by Holland Walk to the west, Duchess of Bedford's Walk to the north, Campden Hill Road to the east and Phillimore Walk to the south. The building agreement was initially for 375 houses on 99-year leases but due to concerns over density in the end 214 houses were built.

The estate is now managed by Savills under the instructions of the Trustees of The Phillimore Estate. Savills are active in maintaining and refurbishing properties owned by the Trustees to a high standard to reflect the styles and tastes of the current market, while retaining the period external facades. Furthermore the estate is actively managed by Savills to maximise returns and enhance values where possible on behalf of the Trustees.

www.phillimore-kensington-estate.co.uk

Below: Phillimore Gardens

Founded: 1717

The Sloane Stanley Estate

The Sloane Stanley Estate was established in 1717 in Chelsea by William Sloane, the elder brother of the more famous Sir Hans Sloane (see The Cadogan Estate; page 60), with the purchase of 47 acres in Chelsea. The land included a farmhouse with closes of arable land and scattered trees, the site of a demolished 17th-century mansion, a new thoroughfare with tenanted dwellings, a piece of vacant ground by the river and a large fruit orchard. Four years later, Sloane bought a further 18 acres, adjacent to the original parcel of land.

In 1821 the estate was inherited by Sloane's grandson Hans, who added the name Stanley after he inherited a number of properties from his late cousin Hans Stanley of Paultons, including 34 acres in the parish of Westminster. The estate then became known as The Sloane Stanley Estate. By the mid-19th century roads had been laid and houses built, from terraced rows with small back yards to handsome villas amid landscaped gardens, along with pubs, shops, a chapel and a school. There were still areas of pasture and land supporting market gardens and plant nurseries.

The Chelsea estate was bounded in the north by Little Chelsea and the Fulham Road, on the east by Upper [Old] Church Street, on the south by the King's Road and Lombard Street [Cheyne Walk], and on the west by what would later be gardens to houses in Limerston Street, Langton Street, Danvers Street and Paultons Square. After World War II, 17 acres were compulsory purchased and by 1962 a further 30 acres had been sold. Further sales were made over the years, some voluntary and some due to leasehold reform. Today the estate is around 10 acres and is focused on mixed commercial and residential blocks on the King's Road and Fulham Road.

In the last decade the Estate has invested in the refurbishment and redevelopment of properties. Over the long term the aim is to retain a balance of use across the estate, and to build a distinct identity for the area.

www.sloanestanley.com

Right: The Bluebird, King's Road

Founded: 1723

The Lowndes Estate

The Lowndes Estate originally comprised two fields, connected by a narrow strip of land now covered by Lowndes Street. The northern field, now occupied by Lowndes Square, was originally in the possession of Westminster Abbey, and contained a copse from which the monks cut their firewood.

William Lowndes, who had been appointed Secretary to the Treasury in 1695, had bought this land by 1723. The development of the neighbouring Grosvenor Estate immediately to the east encouraged his grandson, also named William, to build a residential estate here. He leased the land to Thomas Cubitt, who built the east side of Lowndes Square between 1838 and 1849; the west side was begun in 1844 and the south side developed by Lewis Cubitt. Many of the grand stuccoed terraces, which remain among the most exclusive properties in London, were designed by George Basevi. Many are now individual freeholds.

Right: Chesham Place

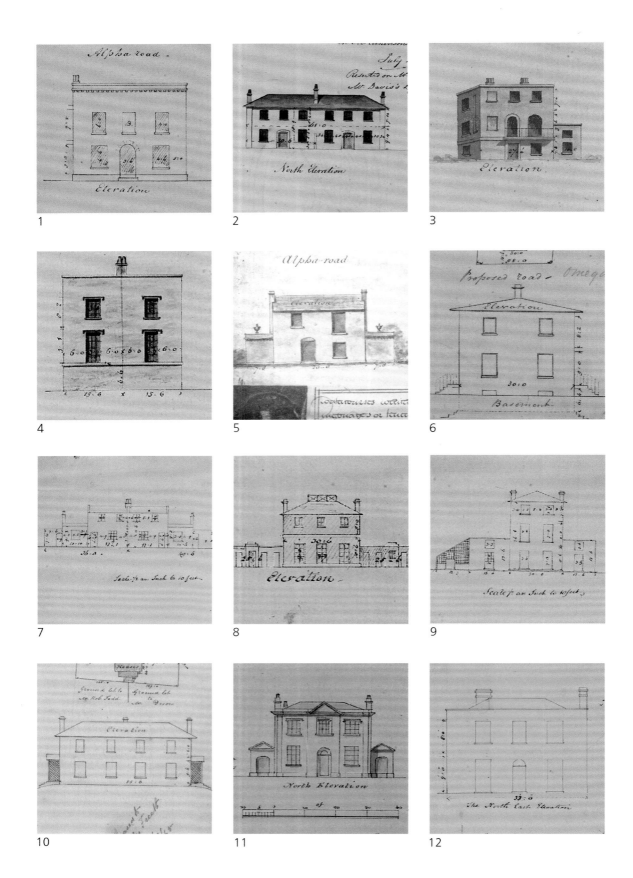

The Eyre Estate

The Eyre Estate in St John's Wood represents a distinct contrast to many of the other original estates, in its architecture, history and evolution. The St John's Wood Estate – originally owned by the Knights of St John of Jerusalem from 1323, hence its name, and then agricultural land – was bought by the Eyre family in 1733. In 1794 a plan was proposed to lay out the estate in a grand circus surrounded by pairs of detached and semi-detached houses, an innovation which set the pattern for much later suburban development. As John Summerson noted in *Georgian London,* this was the first recorded scheme of its kind and the estate became "the first part of London, and indeed of any other town, to abandon the terrace house for the semi-detached villa – a revolution of striking significance and far-reaching effect".

Building began only in 1809 in Alpha Road, on the southern boundary of St John's Wood (demolished with the building of Marylebone Station and its goods yards in 1894), with cottages probably designed to be small second homes for those wishing for a temporary escape from what is now central London. These were followed by a unique pattern of new development in the form of semi-detached Italianate and Gothic villas, creating what was probably the earliest planned suburb anywhere in the world. Several builders took sites, including James Burton and May & Morritt. The then comparatively inexpensive houses, of which there were eventually about 1,500 on 500 acres, attracted authors, artists, philosophers and scientists, including George Eliot and Lawrence Alma-Tadema. Walpole Eyre, the brother of Henry Samuel Eyre, who owned the estate, was the driving force behind the management and development, and oversaw every detail of developers' plans, with both elevations and plans being incorporated into building agreements and ground leases.

In the 1960s, most of St John's Wood was designated a conservation area and its houses were listed, although some houses had been pulled down in the 1920s and 1930s to make way for blocks of flats. However, 90 per cent of properties on the original Eyre Estate are houses – 60 per cent of which are owner-occupied – not flats, and hence the Leasehold Reform Act and the resulting sale of freeholds has had a substantial impact on the estate. Since the mid-1990s a very significant number of the houses have been sold and sales will continue to the extent that the London estate will ultimately be reduced to a small number of properties. The proceeds from sales have been reinvested outside the St John's Wood area.

In 2012, having obtained planning permission for 74 upmarket houses and flats, and 59 affordable homes, The Eyre Estate sold the five-acre site of the 200-year-old St John's Wood barracks when the lease expired. The then occupiers, the King's Troop Royal Horse Artillery, moved to Woolwich.

Left: Elevation drawings of individual Alpha Cottages

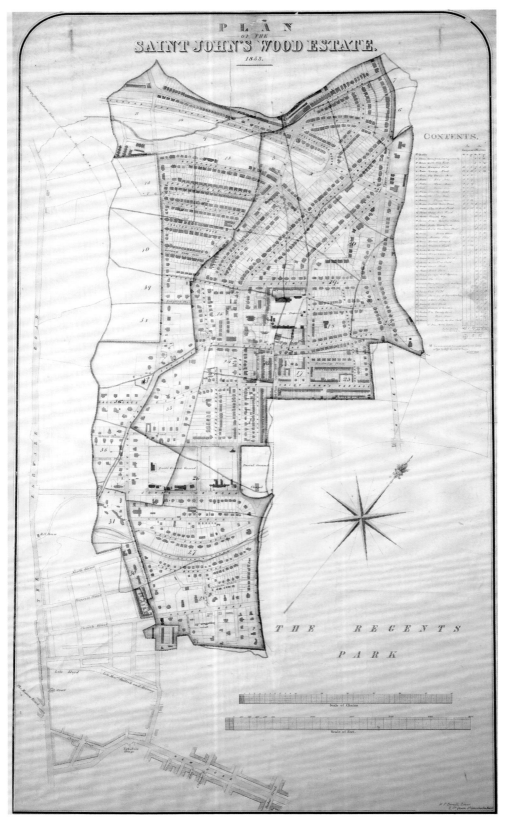

Founded: 1730s

The Berkeley Square Estate

The Berkeley Square Estate takes its name from Lord Berkeley who acquired lands to the north of Piccadilly after the Restoration and built himself a great house (Berkeley House). Berkeley House was later sold to the Duke of Devonshire with the proviso that the view to the north (as far as Lord Berkeley's lands extended) should not be spoiled by having been built on.

The Berkeley family retained much of their original landholdings in the area, and Lord Berkeley's widow, Christian, and her son William, 4th Lord Berkeley, were responsible for leasing the land for the development of housing and defining much of its style and quality. Berkeley Square – on the site of the original gardens north of Berkeley House – was laid out in the 1730s, and the east side was the first to be developed for housing; a few of the houses of this date survive on the west side. The square itself is famed for its 30 plane trees which are said to have been planted in 1789 and are the oldest in London. Many of the properties around the square were sold for redevelopment by the Berkeley family in the 1920s and 1930s as part of the widespread interwar sales of landed estates. Berkeley Square House, built in this period, was until the 1950s one of the largest blocks of shops and offices in Europe.

A portfolio encompassing the Square, Bruton Street and Bruton Place to the east and Hill Street and Charles Street to the west remained in the ownership of the Berkeley family until 1930, when it was sold to Viscount Bearsted. The latter sold it on to the BP Pension Fund managers in the 1960s. In 2001 it was bought by an investment consortium that appointed Lancer Property Asset Management to both manage the estate and make strategic purchases. These included the acquisition of the 1930s Berkeley Square House in 2003 as well as 1 Curzon Street and 50 Berkeley Street. The estate, which is situated in the Mayfair conservation area, is now made up of more than 100 freehold properties in a mix of retail, office and residential, with a number of famous clubs, to a total of in excess of 278,709 sqm. While original facades have been retained, many properties have been refurbished, most recently 22 Hill Street and 41 Berkeley Square, with 34-36 Bruton Street currently underway.

www.berkeleysquareestate.com

Right: Berkeley Square

The Day Estate

The Day Estate in South Kensington covers two portions of land, to the north and south of Old Brompton Road. The Day family first acquired the estate in 1744 when Benjamin Day and his wife Ann inherited the land from Ann's father, Walter Dodemead. Later in the 18th century the northern section of the estate, near Gloucester Road, became the location for five country villas, including Hereford Lodge. In 1819 the estate passed to James Day, who later instigated much of the building development across the estate. The first houses were built in Drayton Gardens and Hereford Square in 1845 and completed during the 1850s. The 18th-century villas surrounding Hereford Square survived until the 1880s when they were demolished to make way for Brechin Place, Rosary Gardens, and Wetherby Place. The estate continues in the hands of a descendant of Benjamin and Ann Day.

Today, The Day Estate is actively managed to maintain and preserve its character and appearance. Enfranchisement proceeds are reinvested into the estate to build upon the residential rental portfolio, replacing lost assets and to ensure the continued success of the estate for future generations of the family.

Below: Drayton Gardens.
Photograph: Agnese Sanvito

The Foundling Hospital Estate

An unusual example of an estate almost created by accident, rather than design, the Foundling Hospital Estate was one of the many estates developed in the Bloomsbury area in the 18th and 19th centuries. It comprised four fields of 56 acres bought by the Governors of the Foundling Hospital – much more than they had wanted, but its owner Lord Salisbury would not part with a smaller site – for building their new home for abandoned children, and the first building phase was completed in 1745. However, this ultimately worked in their favour: when the Hospital faced a lack of funds in the late 18th century, the value of the surrounding pasture land had increased and residential development of the land seemed to be the best option.

Laying out this estate proved more difficult than the Hospital governors had anticipated as it was an isolated site, with the only carriageway into London being Red Lion Street, and development was opposed by wealthy residents in Queen Square and Great Ormond Street, who enjoyed uninterrupted views of green space towards Highgate and Hampstead. Nevertheless, Samuel Pepys Cockerell was appointed architect and surveyor and in 1790 he submitted detailed plans for an entirely residential estate, featuring at the centre two imposing squares (Brunswick and Mecklenburgh Squares) flanking the Hospital gardens and opening towards them, and surrounded by housing for different classes of resident. Development began almost immediately, mainly by James Burton, who took building leases on large parts of the estate from the 1790s onwards and constructed no less than 586 houses. This was the last major estate developed before the outbreak of the Napoleonic Wars in 1793.

Unfortunately in the later 19th century much of the estate became slums and attracted prostitution, hence much demolition and redevelopment took place from the 1870s onwards. In the 1920s the Hospital decided to move to a healthier location in Surrey, and the entire estate was sold to a private contractor in 1925. Residents protested against the developer's proposal to move Covent Garden market to the estate. With the help of the newspaper proprietor Lord Rothermere, seven acres were purchased to be used as a children's playground, as it still is today, known as Coram's Fields. (The Hospital building was nevertheless later demolished.)

The Governors of the Foundling Hospital bought back the north part of the site in 1934 to continue their work, creating what is now the charity Coram (the Thomas Coram Foundation for Children). The Governors also bought back 40 Brunswick Square to serve as its headquarters; this was rebuilt and opened in 1939. This building now houses the Foundling Museum, opened in 2004 and incorporating the boys' staircase and recreating the Court Room, Picture Gallery and Committee Room from the original Hospital.

Right: The Foundling Hospital, Benjamin Cole, 1756 (Etching on paper) © Coram in the care of the Foundling Museum

The Lloyd Baker Estate

The Lloyd Baker Estate, named after the Gloucestershire family who owned it, was one of the architecturally distinctive smaller estates built in Victorian London. The characteristic semidetached, two-storey brick villas with shared pediments, laid out between 1820 and the early 1840s on two adjoining fields on a steep slope between Amwell Street and King's Cross Road, are some of the most elegant examples of small-scale 19th-century housing development.

The estate lies on land once owned by the Knights Hospitallers and through sale was acquired by the Backhouse family, which in the 17th century sold some land on the east side to the New River Company for its reservoir and 'water house', New River Head (see page 83). Ultimately it passed to Dr William Lloyd, Bishop of St Asaph's. In 1775 his great-granddaughter married the Rev William Baker and the land formed part of her dowry. It was the Rev Baker who from 1819, with his son Thomas Lloyd Baker, developed the land, then known as Black Mary's Field and Robin Hood's Field, with a circus, square and terraces designed by John and William Joseph Booth.

The estate continued in the family's hands until the death in 1975 of Olive Lloyd Baker, who became a well-known figure in the local area, regularly visiting her tenants. The estate sold 95 houses to Islington Council (on Granville Square, Wharton Street and the north side of Lloyd Baker Street), but some 40 properties were retained, mostly flats. Lloyd Square remained as leasehold in private ownership, and a garden committee run by residents has managed the square's garden, the layout of which remains relatively intact, since 1917.

Above and right: Lloyd Square

Founded: 1799

The Gunter Estate

The Gunter Estate was somewhat different to many of the original London estates as it was bought and built by a confectioner, James Gunter, in the 18th century. Gunter began buying farmland piecemeal in what is now Earls Court from 1799 so that he could establish a market gardening business. (He also bought Earls Court Lodge which was named 'Current Jelly Hall' by its disdainful neighbours.)

Between 1808 and 1810 he built some villas in the corner of Earls Court Road and Old Brompton Road and south of Old Brompton Road to the west of Coleherne House. These were all later demolished as the estate was more intensively developed by his descendants for more intensive building of residential terraces, in particular what was known as the Redcliffe Estate, constructed from 1864 to 1878 by William Corbett and Alexander McClymont. The Gunter Estate remained in the ownership of the family until 2002, when it was sold to a private investor.

Below: No. 29 Ashburn Place, elevation, 1882–3. Courtesy of Survey of London

Founded: 1807
[Hyde Park Estate]

The Church Commissioners – Hyde Park Estate

The Church Commissioners, established in 1948 from the merger of two much earlier bodies, the Ecclesiastical Commissioners (est. 1836) and Queen Anne's Bounty (est. 1704), is responsible for an investment portfolio of £5.5 billion derived from the Church of England's historic resources. Two of the key aims of the Commissioners are to support the nationwide ministry of the Church, particularly in areas of need and opportunity, and to pay for all clergy pensions earned up to 1998.

The property investment portfolio comprises one-third of their total fund and was valued in December 2012 at over £1.8 billion. It is spread across a range of sectors and regions, including residential, commercial and rural land holdings throughout the UK, as well as in specialist indirect property funds, both here and overseas. (This includes a large share of The Pollen Estate [see page 44], encompassing office and retail properties around New Bond Street, Cork Street and Savile Row.)

The Church Commissioners seek the best long-term financial return from their investments, and aim for at least inflation plus five per cent. Asset management and investment strategies are in accordance with ethical investment policies. In London The Church Commissioners traditionally held predominantly residential property, on the Hyde Park Estate, in Maida Vale and the 'Octavia Hill' Estates both north and south of the river. In 2005-6 they sold a number of residential estates in order to manage their investment exposure to residential property.

Today the residential portfolio is concentrated on the Hyde Park Estate, which

Below: Estate map, 20th century lease holdings

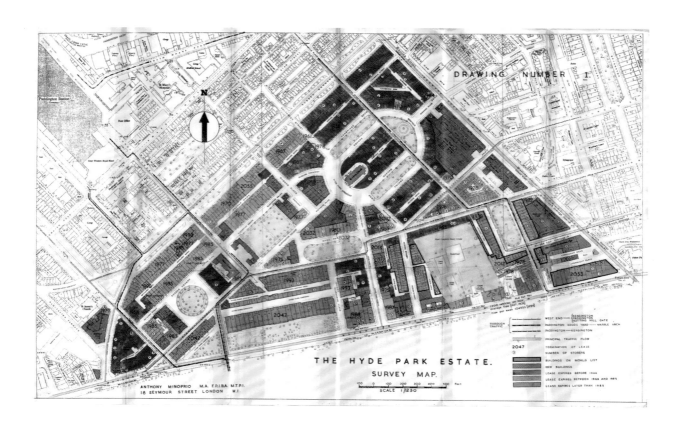

consists of 1,800 freehold and long leasehold properties, with another 40 properties spread across Maida Vale, Chelsea and Westminster. The estate, developed from 1807, runs from Marble Arch along the Bayswater Road to Lancaster Gate and along Sussex Gardens to Edgware Road. It originally belonged to the Bishop of London before being transferred to the Ecclesiastical Commissioners in 1836. The area was significantly redeveloped with larger modern blocks in the 1950s and 1960s and a new phase focused on conservation began in the 1970s.

As well as the London Lancaster Hotel, the Hyde Park Estate has a number of shops, restaurants and galleries centred on Connaught Village. This is the estate's retail heart. The Church Commissioners have been undertaking a policy of active management and refurbishment to create a distinctive, premier retail quarter offering independent retail, particularly women's fashion and vintage couture, dining, and local shops.

The Estate has the ambition to be the greenest in London: current initiatives include improvement of green spaces through revamping many of the gardens and specifically introducing native species, with a newly installed estate greenhouse in Devonport Gardens and plans to introduce olive trees for property frontages. As well as making public spaces more attractive and enhancing biodiversity, insect hotels, bird and bat boxes have been installed in gardens across the estate and an eco pond established.

Recent public realm improvements include the establishment of the Hyde Park Estate brand which now features on the improved and harmonised signage across

Below: The Water Gardens, 1967, Trehearne & Norman and Preston & Partners

the estate. This helps to promote the estate's location and give a sense of 'place' for the residents. Iron railings are planned to be reinstated on Sussex Gardens and Hyde Park Square, as well as cast iron bollards featuring the Hyde Park brand in Sussex Gardens.

A major recent project, completed in 2012, was the £10 million conversion of The Brassworks, a remodelling by Belsize Architects of a former Victorian brass instrument factory into eight contemporary loft-style apartments, within a conservation area. The focus of the project was a new landscaped central courtyard with a bronze sculpture and waterfall into a pond. This retained original features while creating fashionable, minimalist spaces. The scheme restored the original facade, and opened up the arches on the ground floor with steel gates featuring a brass tubing motif, referring to the building's original use. One flat on the ground floor has irregular walls, an internal glazed courtyard and a sunken media room. From the first floor upwards, the U-shaped layout of the building has been exploited to form two flats at each level, with views onto the internal courtyard. In line with The Church Commissioners' sustainability strategy, the building incorporates a green roof.

www.churchofengland.org; www.hydeparkestate.com

Above: The Brassworks, exterior
Right: The Brassworks, interior

Founded: 1821

The Benyon Estate (De Beauvoir)

The Benyon Estate is a fine example of a Victorian estate in Hackney and has remained in the ownership of the Benyon family since it was built. It consists of about 300 properties – mostly flats, maisonettes and houses, but also with some retail, office and industrial units – located within the conservation area of De Beauvoir Town. It is bounded by Kingsland Road to the east, Buckingham Road to the north, Southgate Road to the west and the Regent's Canal to the south. The name De Beauvoir derives from Richard De Beauvoir who bought the Balmes Estate, a farm and manor house on this site, in 1640.

The impetus for development in the area came from the cutting of the Regent's Canal in 1812 and the urbanisation of the areas to the north and east of the City in the early and mid-19th century, and the subsequent demand for housing. In 1821 a 99 year building lease on 150 acres of land – reputedly the largest single area given to a speculative builder in London – was granted to a tenant farmer, William Rhodes, by Peter de Beauvoir, who died in the same year. Peter's nearest relative, a clergyman named Richard Benyon, inherited ownership of the land and adopted the De Beauvoir name, though the development of the estate became a matter of protracted legal disputes between Benyon and Rhodes.

Rhodes's original design, on a grid pattern, encompassed four squares on diagonal streets intersecting at an octagon. After Richard Benyon de Beauvoir gained direct control of development in 1834, a more spacious layout of small terraces and semidetached villas was preferred; of Rhodes' proposed squares only the southeast one, now De Beauvoir Square, was built although the diagonals partly survived in Enfield, Stamford, and Ardleigh roads.

Today all the residential properties are offered on shorthold tenancies and the Estate manages and delivers an ongoing programme of refurbishment and maintenance. It has also commissioned from Henley Halebrown Rorrison a £9.5 million residential-led, mixed-use project overlooking the Regent's Canal to create 35 new homes, including four triplex flats, as well as a new pub, shop, two cafés, office space and new piazzas linking Kingsland Road to the waterfront. The design was inspired by the Uffizi Palace in Florence, with colonnades lining the basin square.

www.benyonestate.com

Right: Semidetached villa near De Beauvoir Square.
Photograph: Agnese Sanvito

Founded: 1829

The Maryon Wilson Estate

The development of the Maryon Wilson Estate in Hampstead was part of the vast expansion of building into the environs of London during the 19th century and the growth of suburban speculative development. Its origins can be traced to the ancient manor of Hampstead, bought in 1707 by Sir Thomas Langhorne of Charlton, Kent, a rich merchant and former Governor of Madras. In 1829 his distant relative, Sir Thomas Maryon Wilson, the later owner of the estate, petitioned Parliament to let him build on Hampstead Heath but building work was put on hold owing to protests by local residents and a subsequent lawsuit, unresolved at his death in 1869.

In 1871 the Metropolitan Board of Works took possession of the Heath and it was sold by the family at full market value (then £47,000). From the 1870s to 1914 new roads and estates south and west of Hampstead Village were constructed on the estate, among the most notable of which is Fitzjohn's Avenue with its distinctive red-brick gabled houses. In 1972 some freeholds were sold to Bryston Property Group. The estate is now owned by Viscount Gough and managed by Farebrother.

The family also owned Charlton House in south-east London, where they lived until 1916. It was sold to Greenwich Council in 1925.

Below: Fitzjohns Avenue.
Photograph: Agnese Sanvito

Founded: 1853

The Royal Commission for the Exhibition of 1851

Unlike most other historic estates, the origins of The Royal Commission for the Exhibition of 1851 lie in a specific event rather than in acquisition of land or property by an individual or family. The Commission was established in 1850 to organise and stage the Great Exhibition of 1851 in Hyde Park, with land acquired in 1853.

The Exhibition, housing over 100,000 exhibits in Joseph Paxton's iconic Crystal Palace, was enormously successful, attracting six million visitors in under six months. After it closed the Commission remained as a charitable institution intended to "increase the means of industrial education and extend the influence of science and art upon productive industry". With the £186,000 surplus generated by the Exhibition, together with further funding from Parliament it bought 87 acres of land, principally market gardens in South Kensington. Initially land was leased to the Royal Horticultural Society to create large formal gardens, surrounded by exhibition galleries and, to the north, the Central Hall of Art and Science (renamed the Royal Albert Hall by Queen Victoria) which opened in 1871. Land was also made available for the building of what became the Victoria and Albert Museum, the Natural History Museum and later the Science Museum. The Royal Horticultural Society surrendered their lease in 1878, making way for the Royal College of Science, The Royal School of Mines, the City and Guilds Technical College and the Imperial Institute all of which became Imperial College in 1907. The Royal Colleges of Art and Music were also established in this period. By 1891, there were sufficient funds for The Royal Commission to set up an educational trust. It supports research in science and engineering, applied research in industry, industrial design and other projects by providing grants. Today, the Commission has capital assets of over £80 million and its total annual grants amount to £2 million.

The key principle in the management of the estate today is to continue to enhance its status as a globally important centre for culture and research and to promote it as a renowned cultural quarter to visitors. In February 2010 architectural practice DSDHA was awarded the Research Fellowship in the Built Environment by the Commission, which supported an intensive research programme to develop a long-term vision for the estate, specifically the area around the Royal Albert Hall.

Studies revealed the practical need to improve the visitor experience around the Hall and northwards across Kensington Gore to the Albert Memorial. DSDHA are therefore planning and implementing a programme of improvements to a network of pedestrian routes and interconnections, working in conjunction with Allies and Morrison Urban Practitioners.

www.royalcommission1851.org.uk

Right: Crystal Palace, 1851

Founded: 1883
[Peabody founded 1862]

Peabody: The Whitecross Street Estate

Peabody is one of London's largest and oldest housing associations, with a well-established public profile as a charitable organisation and a distinctive architectural and social heritage. Peabody was founded as the Peabody Donation Fund in 1862 by the American banker and philanthropist George Peabody. He was concerned by the poverty that he saw in his adopted home of London, and during his lifetime he donated £500,000 to the trustees of the Fund to "ameliorate the conditions of the poor and needy of London". This, he suggested, should be achieved by "the construction of such improved dwellings for the poor as may combine in the utmost possible degree the essentials of healthfulness, comfort, social enjoyment and economy".

Peabody's first period of development took place between 1864 and 1890, with architect Henry Darbishire and contractors William Cubitt & Co. building the characteristic 'Peabody estates' known today. The first, built at a cost of £22,000, was in Commercial Street, Spitalfields, and opened in 1864, followed by estates in Islington, Shadwell, Chelsea, Southwark, Blackfriars Road and other locations. Until 1900 Peabody was limited to building within an eight-mile radius from the Royal Exchange in the City of London. In the 1870s and 1880s the organisation bought sites from the Metropolitan Board of Works, which had itself compulsorily purchased the land from a variety of owners under one of London's first slum clearance schemes. Peabody's return on capital only had to be three per cent, unlike five per cent for most comparable organisations at the time, which enabled it to begin development on a large scale.

The Whitecross estate in Islington was the 16th and largest of these original Peabody estates, built in 1883 to the north of Barbican. Whitecross actually consisted of two estates, always considered as one entity. The Whitecross Street estate itself contained 22 blocks on the east side of Whitecross Street between Roscoe Street and Errol Street, including three blocks at the east end of Dufferin Street. The smaller Roscoe Street estate consisted of 11 blocks to the west of Whitecross Street, and one to the east. When first built, the estate reportedly housed 4,000 people.

The health of the tenants was a key factor in the design of Peabody homes, so standalone blocks of five or six storeys provided good ventilation and daylighting, and surrounded a courtyard where children could play. This pattern was followed at Whitecross, as was the distinctive use of yellow brick. The flats were built in a style known as 'associated dwellings' with shared sinks and WCs on the landings that could be inspected regularly. Like many estates, Roscoe Street had shared laundry provision as well as a coal store and pramsheds, but (unlike others) there were no baths or hot water.

Below: George Peabody

Each Peabody estate originally had a resident superintendent, who collected rents and enforced rules such as cleaning of communal facilities and sweeping passages, and several porters. This hands-on approach to management remains in place today: all estates, including Whitecross Street, have a Neighbourhood Manager whose duties include tenancy audits, regular estate walkabouts, engaging with the tenants' association and addressing low-level antisocial behaviour.

The outbreak of the Second World War brought a halt to Peabody's building across London. The Whitecross Street area was badly affected by the Blitz in 1940–41 and many buildings were damaged beyond repair. Of the original Roscoe Street estate, six blocks were burnt out in an air raid in December 1940, and two others destroyed in 1941.

The Peabody Donation Fund Act, a private Act of Parliament, was passed in 1948, and was partly intended to give Peabody the powers it needed to complete its post-war recovery programme; £1 million of modernisation took place across

Top: The Whitecross Estate
Left: Alyne House

London during the 1950s and was grant-funded by the Government.

In the 1950s Peabody rebuilt the Roscoe Street estate using additional land compulsorily acquired by the London County Council (LCC). The land had previously been the site of St Mary's Church, built in 1868 and later demolished after war damage, and two burial grounds, closed in the 19th century. This redevelopment, designed by John Grey and Partner, consisted of two 13-storey blocks and three lower buildings. The tower blocks are believed to be the first blocks of that height in London that were permitted to be built with a single staircase. Banner House was built in 1972 when the remaining four Victorian blocks were demolished.

The original blocks on the Whitecross Street estate were also renovated, in particular blocks H and K, which were converted in 1993 to provide sheltered housing for elderly people and are now known collectively as Alleyn House. In 1967 Peabody also acquired and incorporated into the Whitecross Street estate the LCC's early housing property, Dufferin Dwellings. This block of flats was built in 1898 to provide housing for costermongers with stables/sheds below for their carts and ponies.

Today Peabody owns or manages more than 20,000 properties across 30 London boroughs, housing nearly 55,000 people in more than 200 locations. The organisation's mission remains at the core of its work, with its key principles being to ensure that as many people as possible have 'a good home, a real sense of purpose and a strong feeling of belonging'. Peabody also recognises that providing someone in need with a home is not enough: its well-established and large-scale community programme offers help with employment and training, volunteering schemes and activities for young people, for example.

In 2007 Peabody launched 'Improve', a ten-year programme that aims to transform the open spaces around its estates. Whitecross, like other Peabody estates, has a significant amount of hard landscaping, including parking areas, but also areas with no defined uses. In 2010 the independent public realm and urban design consultancy Publica was commissioned by the local tenants' association to help identify and articulate residents' concerns and aspirations for the estate's public spaces, with the aim of creating a shared vision and clear principles for future regeneration. A masterplan is now being drawn up.

In addition, Peabody is exploring the potential of developing new homes on its existing estates to meet the pressing demand for affordable housing, and has investigated building on under-utilised land or garage sites at Whitecross Street. In 2010 it commissioned Riches Hawley Mikhail Architects to generate options for town houses and maisonette-type accommodation to replace existing garages to the rear of the block on Dufferin Street.

——
www.peabody.org.uk

Founded: 19th century

The New River Estate

The New River Estate was an unusual example of a 19th-century estate linked to the development of London's water supply infrastructure. The New River was originally a 38-mile man-made watercourse bringing fresh water into London from the springs of Hertfordshire, terminating at the New River Head waterworks and reservoirs in Clerkenwell. The New River Company, which owned the land, saw steadily increasing profits in the 17th and 18th centuries, and as a result acquired property in an area of open fields, ponds and springs presently bordered by St John Street, Pentonville Road, King's Cross Road and Rosebery Avenue. William Chadwell Mylne, the company surveyor laid out the streets and squares of fine stock-brick houses, including Myddelton and Claremont Squares, and one circus, in the 1820s.

In the 1970s, the company was taken over by London Merchant Securities, and most of the estate, apart from some commercial properties off Rosebery Avenue and three parts of Myddleton Square, was sold to Islington Council. The former headquarters of the company, built in 1920, has been converted to 129 flats by the Manhattan Loft Corporation and Berkeley Homes.

Right: View of the area around New River Head, Finsbury 1665. Courtesy of the London Metropolitan Archives

Hampstead Garden Suburb

Hampstead Garden Suburb was the culmination of the ideals of the Victorian and Edwardian philanthropists who aimed to create well-designed new communities with clean air and green space. Situated between Golders Green and East Finchley, it was begun in 1907 by Henrietta Barnett. She and her husband, Canon Samuel Barnett, had between them established a number of charitable and educational institutions in Whitechapel, including Toynbee Hall.

When the extension of the Underground railway north to Golders Green was planned, Mrs Barnett organised the purchase of Wyldes Farm (an estate of 323 acres owned by Eton College; see page 30), part of which was to form an extension to Hampstead Heath. The remainder was to form a residential area as a pleasant and healthy place for people of all walks of life to live in. The suburb was planned by Raymond Unwin and Barry Parker, who had designed Letchworth Garden City in 1903. Other architects, in particular Sir Edwin Lutyens, were commissioned to design individual houses and flats, laid out in tree-lined roads. To the north was social housing for the elderly, orphans and other needy groups and cottages for artisans, while houses for the middle classes lay mainly to the east and larger villas and mansions for the wealthy to the south.

The suburb, covering 320 hectares and home to 13,000 residents, is now recognised as one of the best examples of early 20th-century residential architecture, landscape and planning, and as such was designated a conservation area in 1969. In 1974 the High Court authorised a Scheme under which all householders must obtain the Trust's approval before altering the external appearance of their properties. In 2010 a £6 million refurbishment and new extension by Hopkins Architects to the Henrietta Barnett School in the Suburb was completed. The main building of the school, which was founded in 1911, is a Lutyens-designed Grade II* listed building. The scheme provided an additional 1200 sqm of teaching rooms, including two new buildings for music/drama and art/design and technology.

www.hgstrust.org

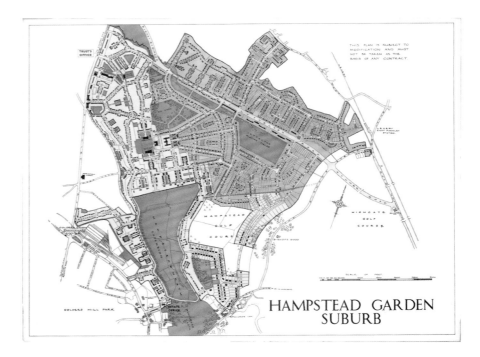

HAMPSTEAD GARDEN SUBURB

Right: Estate map, 1936

Founded: 1925

The Langham Estate

The Langham Estate consists of 13.8 acres in the West End, from Oxford Street to the south and Euston Road to the north. It was originally part of the land owned by the Earl of Oxford, which was inherited by the family of Lord Howard de Walden (see page 57) in the late 19th century, but sold by the family in 1925 to Sir John Ellerman. It then passed through several owners until it was bought in 1994 by the current owners, Mount Eden Land Limited. It now has an eclectic mix of tenants ranging from major retail chains to galleries, restaurants, fashion showrooms, and medical and educational organisations, and creative and media businesses.

www.langhamestate.com

Right: Great Portland Street

Founded: 1974

The Knightsbridge Estate

The Knightsbridge Estate is a 3.5 acre island site bounded by Sloane Street to the north, Brompton Road to the west, Hans Crescent to the south and Basil Street to the east. Previously owned by BP Pension (Ropemaker) Fund and sold to a private overseas investor for just over £500 million in 2010, the estate comprises 520,000 sq ft of retail, office, residential and hotel space in one of London's most prestigious and high-profile shopping areas, and is flanked by Harvey Nichols and Harrods. The estate is now owned by the Olayan Group and asset managed in its entirety by Chelsfield.

There are 40 buildings on the estate, all mostly dating from 1880, and since 2010 the estate has been employed in refurbishing properties and on repositioning through a development of a cohesive brand as a luxury retail destination creating a natural link between Harvey Nichols and Harrods. Over the past three years there have been more than 70 lettings and the percentage of premium retailers has increased from 26 per cent to 76 per cent. The Estate has also sought to improve the public realm through a £2.5 million lighting scheme and programme of facade cleaning, pavement widening and landscaping in keeping with the area.

Below: Brompton Road and Sloane Street

www.knightsbridge-estate.com

THE NEWER ESTATES

The examples set by the original estates are being emulated by landowners who recognise the benefits of long termism and place management.

Founded: 1970s

Soho Estates

Soho Estates, created from the property acquisitions of Paul Raymond in and around Soho, has been described as the 'next great landed estate', and, like the original estates founded long before it, is managed in such a way as to ensure that it endures for the long term.

The estate covers large parts of Soho's 87 acres, including Soho Square to Dean Street and most of Old Compton Street – as well as the north side of Leicester Square – and the owners are in the process of acquisition to fill the gaps between its holdings. Soho Estates began as a collection of historic buildings acquired from the 1970s to the 1990s – when there was a low level of competition for the purchase of buildings – by the club owner, pornographer and entrepreneur Paul Raymond, sometimes known as 'the King of Soho'. His Raymond Revuebar opened in Soho in 1958 and he reportedly chose to invest the profits from his entertainment and publishing ventures in properties within five minutes' walk of where he was based. The properties were bought from a wide range of different owners. On his death in 2008, ownership passed to his two granddaughters and the estate is held in trust for them. In 2012 it was valued at £329 million.

Raymond's approach was to buy individual buildings and rent them out rather than invest in updating existing buildings because he preferred simply to concentrate on buying more. This resulted in a well-managed but under-utilised estate with the upper levels of many buildings vacant or in a state of disrepair. Most of the estate consists of buildings constructed between 1700 and 1850 (the oldest building dates from 1695), many of which are not fit for purpose. Thus it differs from the original estates (and many of the contemporary ones) in being founded on the acquisition of existing structures, rather than creating a new area on a blank canvas.

The estate is 'passionate' about the heritage and history of Soho, and its motto is to 'Keep Soho's soul'. Soho itself was an area that traditionally had a fragmented ownership – parts of the land were granted, leased or sold by the Crown from the 16th century onwards to a variety of people including the Earls of Portland, Newport, Leicester and Salisbury – and was developed piecemeal after the Great Fire. In the 1670s and 1680s building progressed rapidly as the area became a haven for artists and for French Huguenot craftsmen and tradesmen, exiled from their homeland because of their Protestant religion. In the 19th century the area had the highest density of population of anywhere in London, and as the wealthier families moved away, it consolidated its reputation as a place for entertainment and theatres, and, in the 20th century, restaurants and later the sex industry.

The strategy of the business now is to enhance and add value to existing stock through careful restoration and refurbishment, and, where possible, redevelopment in keeping with the area. Most of the estate's tenants are restaurants, bars and clubs,

Below: Paul Raymond

along with some hotels, retail on Old Compton Street, and residential units rented on short-term tenancies. The area's identity is built largely around its night-time economy and historic reputation as an area where entrepreneurs have started up new businesses. There is also a strong sense of community, which the Estate seeks to support through providing funding to local charities such as Centrepoint and the House of St Barnabas, as well as Soho Parish School. Keeping the vibrancy and unique, edgy character of the area is a key priority, and Crossrail is expected to provide a major rejuvenation in terms of bringing in visitors from the north-east, when traditionally they have travelled to Soho via Piccadilly Circus or Leicester Square.

Recent projects have included Bateman Street, Old Compton Street, Archer Street, Wardour Street, Winnett Street, and major work to refurbish 76 Dean Street, a Grade II*-listed property gutted by a massive fire in 2009 but still with an important 18th-century seascape mural going up the staircase. This Georgian structure was built in 1732 as a town house for First Lord of the Fleet John Hamilton, before becoming a leather factory and later a children's home and office accommodation, and is being restored to its original use. A recent purchase was 5 Richmond Mews, which lies to the rear at 76 Dean Street, and is being incorporated into the redevelopment by SODA Architects to create a 20,000 sq ft private members club for the Soho House Group.

In 2012 Soho Estates acquired for £74 million the 125,000 sq ft Foyles portfolio, covering the Foyles Building over one acre of land between Charing Cross Road and Greek Street. The famous bookstore will relocate to an adjacent purpose-built property, part of the redevelopment of the former Central St Martin's Building at 107-109 Charing Cross Road. The Charing Cross Road elevation will be retained for retail and the Greek Street site as a mixed-use development and the project overall will benefit from its location next to Crossrail, which will change the footfall of the area.

The Estate also proposes to redevelop Walkers Court, a narrow pedestrianised street between Brewer Street and Peter Street. It links Rupert Street with Berwick Street, which is popular with tourists and the local workers and works as a north-south connecting route to and from the heart of the West End. The £45 million project, submitted for planning in July 2013, will incorporate a restaurant and Soho Estates' new offices, and will include the resurrection of the Boulevard Theatre.

www.sohoestates.co.uk

Right: Walkers Court, Matt Architecture / soda

Right: Dean Street.
Photograph: Agnese Sanvito
Below: 76 Dean Street
exterior, soda
Below right: 76 Dean Street
interior, soda

Founded: 1982

Broadgate

Broadgate, jointly owned by British Land and Blackstone, is a fully managed commercial estate, first built in the 1980s, covering 30 acres around Liverpool Street Station, with 16 buildings set around four landscaped squares and more than 60 restaurants, bars, shops and health clubs. It was the largest office development in London before the building of Canary Wharf in the 1990s but has been progressively developed and adapted for changing business needs. It now provides 4.4 million sq ft of office space with a further 700,000 sq ft under development.

Broadgate, developed by Rosehaugh but later acquired by British Land (which sold a 50 per cent share to Blackstone in 2009), was one of the most innovative developments of its type and period, as well as being the largest and most ambitious building project in the City, and is widely regarded as a model of best practice in the development of new estates, although in many ways its inspiration came from North America rather than the great estates of London.

It was the result of a major transformation of the financial services industry after deregulation of the stock market in the 1980s. At this time advances in IT meant that financial trading companies no longer needed to be physically located near to the Stock Exchange in the City, as they had traditionally been. Research for the new development demonstrated that large floorplates, high performance equipment and space to conceal thousands of miles of cabling, as well as convenient public transport, were required, in buildings that could operate 24 hours a day in response to the increased activity following deregulation.

Below: Exchange Square, SOM

The new development was situated on the original site of Broad Street station

Below: 5 Broadgate,
Make Architects

(closed in 1986) and beside and above the railway approaches into Liverpool Street station. The first phase of building began in 1982 with 1 Finsbury Avenue, then let on a 30-year lease to UBS. Phases 1-4, including nos. 1-2, 3, 4, 6 and 8-12 Broadgate and 100 Liverpool Street, continued through 1985 to 1987. The early buildings were designed by Peter Foggo, then of Arup Associates, which was also responsible for the overall masterplan of the site.

The planning and layout of the development are widely regarded as the most significant factors in the success of the scheme, and in this respect do bear striking similarities to the principles applied in the original estates in terms of creating a new part of the city that over time integrates organically with the whole. Foggo's team undertook a careful analysis of pedestrian movements through the areas, and the buildings were located in such a way as to slot into the existing urban grain and street plan in the area around Liverpool Street. New frontages were created in backland areas behind the overall frontage onto Liverpool Street, with the aim of drawing people into the area.

Perhaps most importantly, the buildings were surrounded by open spaces and public art, such as Richard Serra's *Fulcrum*, with interweaving pedestrian routes. Broadgate was among the first examples in the UK that drew on the mid-20th-century North American model of a privately owned but publicly accessible urban 'estate', combining large volumes of speculative office space with landscaped public areas served by shops, cafés and restaurants. The Broadgate Circle, built in 1987–8, was revolutionary at the time in its provision of events and public facilities, including an ice rink.

As in the case of the original estates, it is the overall quality of the environment that has ensured its resilience and growth, based on the mix of different types of buildings, animated public space, easily accessible transport – Crossrail is expected to generate a potential 30 per cent increase in footfall – and careful maintenance, management and provision of high-quality services to occupiers, provided by Broadgate Estates (a subsidiary of British Land). Today, Broadgate remains a dynamic business community, with over 30,000 workers. Unlike the original estates, the public spaces are privately managed, and thus more control is possible.

As Broadgate matured, it generated enormous value to the surrounding area and thus has been an engine of regeneration for the northern fringe of the City. Greater emphasis is being placed on building up relationships with technology companies, clustered in and around Shoreditch, and on diversifying the occupier mix from purely financial services; originally buildings were let to a single occupier over 25-30 years, but there are now more multi-let buildings on shorter terms of 10 years. To provide the best occupier experience at any time of day and to maintain the high number of occupiers who stay for the long term, as well as social interaction, Broadgate has aimed to provide a diverse programme of events to enliven the public spaces, including large screens relaying sporting and other major events, artisan markets, retail promotions and a diverse retail offer; these are all supported online by a dedicated website and social media. The Broadgate team is also actively involved in a range of community projects with local partners, including provision of jobs for local unemployed people. Recent projects have included Broadgate Stories, a free app on art and architecture across the estate created by young people from Hackney seeking employment in the creative and digital sectors, and concluded at an event held at the recently opened Broadgate Welcome Centre.

Nearly half of Broadgate has been recently developed, refurbished or is under construction, and occupancy remains high. More than £40 million has also been spent on improving the public spaces, particularly around Exchange Square. In response to the need for office spaces that are flexible and sustainable, the most recent newly built addition, The Broadgate Tower, completed in 2008 alongside 201 Bishopsgate, offers smaller floorplates to attract smaller firms. Major investment was made in landscaping the surrounding area, including the creation of a large plaza to the front of The Broadgate Tower, which adds to Broadgate's vibrant squares and open spaces. At the time this was the largest speculative office development in London. 199 Bishopsgate was also recently refurbished by John Robertson Architects to provide 146,000 sq ft of Grade A office space and improve environmental performance from a standard fit for the 1990s to BREEAM Excellent rating, reducing carbon emissions by 60 per cent. British Land has also instigated a programme to reduce energy use across the estate.

More recently the largest ever pre-let in the City Corporation area was secured with UBS signing up to a 700,000 sq ft scheme at 5 Broadgate designed by Make Architects, due for shell and core completion in 2015. The 12-storey building will include up to four trading floors, each able to accommodate approximately 750 traders, allowing UBS to consolidate its London trading operations under one roof. The development also includes public realm and landscaping enhancements from Sun Street Passage to Primrose Street, and allows for the introduction of retail space in the new Sun Street Square. Planning consent has recently been granted for a £20 million upgrade to the public space and retail and restaurant offer at The Broadgate Circle, which is currently on site and expected to complete in 2015 and with an expanded range of events to create the pre-eminent leisure, retail and food destination in the City.

———
www.broadgate.co.uk

Founded: 1984

Regent's Place

Regent's Place, owned and developed by British Land, is a mixed-use business, retail and residential quarter, or campus, on the north side of Euston Road. As a 13 acre, fully managed campus in London's West End, it is currently occupied by nearly 12,000 workers and residents.

The property has been in the British Land portfolio since 1984 but was developed from the 1990s onwards, building on the company's experience of creating Broadgate in the City, and applying the practice and knowledge learned from that development in public realm improvements, occupier service provision, community relations and integration into the wider urban landscape to create an integrated campus that is now the company's major asset in the West End. Like Broadgate, Regent's Place is also managed by Broadgate Estates, enabling a consistency of approach across British Land's major London assets.

Regent's Place was developed by British Land from an earlier speculative development of the 1960s and 1970s, the Euston Centre, which included at its southeast corner the 34-storey Euston Tower, one of the first high-rise office developments in the West End. Work by British Land began in 1996 and involved the demolition of the head office and studios of Thames Television and the subsequent development

Right: Aerial view of the campus

Right: 10 Brock Street,
Wilkinson Eyre Architects

of the central part of the site and much of the Euston Road frontage, with four new office buildings and a pedestrian plaza called Triton Square.

One building, 2-3 Triton Square, was designed by Sheppard Robson and completed in 2002 as a new headquarters for Abbey National (now Santander UK). The main atrium is 35 metres wide and was reportedly the largest atrium over a trading floor in Europe at the time of occupation. The lower levels of Euston Tower were remodelled at the same time. British Land also invested in the quality of the public realm by commissioning leading artists including a landmark large mural by Michael Craig-Martin, a lighting scheme by Liam Gillick, and a sculptural installation by Antony Gormley.

Regent's Place over has been transformed over the last eight years in order to create a more cohesive place. Key to this was the purchase of the western end from The Crown Estate in 2005 – then occupied by poorer quality office space – and the development of 10 and 20 Triton Street, completed in 2009. In addition 350 Euston Road, designed by Sheppard Robson, was a part of a move to provide more multi-occupancy space in response to changing demands and demographics.

The advantages of a dedicated management team, an essential element now established on many estates, both original and more recently established, enables the estate owner to provide costs savings on mechanical and engineering contracts, cleaning and estate-wide security. Alongside this the growing demand from occupiers for total occupancy costs has led to a strong focus on exploring ways of reducing energy demand, and therefore costs, across Regent's Place, an approach also

implemented at Broadgate. 10 and 20 Triton Street, which both achieved **BREEAM**
Excellent sustainability ratings, incorporate a rainwater harvesting system that saves
2.4 million litres of water every year, for example; landlord-influenced energy use
at Regent's Place has also been cut by 33 per cent across all like-for-like buildings,
saving occupiers more than £500,000 and reducing carbon emissions by 4,200
tonnes. British Land is also working with six occupiers at Regent's Place to reduce
carbon emissions from energy use in both common parts and occupied areas. Free
Wi-Fi has also been implemented across the estate as it has been at Broadgate.

Regent's Place is an evolution of British Land's pioneering approach to the
management of privately owned public space. At the heart is the Plaza, surrounded
by restaurants and cafes and a place where occupiers meet, eat and drink. The on-
site management team devises and manages an annual events programme, including
big screens, theatre, farmers' markets and music.

Regent's Place is directly located between Great Portland Street and Warren
Street underground stations but pedestrian access across Euston Road was
limited and the link to Regent's Park indistinct. To improve its connections to the
surrounding areas, a new west-to-east walkway was created across the estate from
Regent's Park to Euston Station, opening up the historic facade of Holy Trinity
Church, and a new pedestrian crossing inserted in the Euston Road (the first in ten
years) to make it easier for people to reach Fitzrovia, tube stations and the West
End. Carmody Groake's Regent's Place Pavilion (2007) provides a new landmark
entrance to the estate. Investment into new community facilities includes an 80-seat
community theatre, the New Diorama Theatre, as well as arts events and workshops
for local schoolchildren, including annual projects for them to work with artists
on sculptural pieces inspired by the local environment and displayed in the public
spaces.

The final phase of development includes 10 and 30 Brock Street, the Triton
Building and 175 Drummond Street, providing 500,000 sq ft of office, residential
and retail space. 10 Brock Street, completed in summer 2013, will provide
320,000 sq ft of offices designed by Wilkinson Eyre Architects. The ground to fifth
floors have been pre-let to Debenhams plc for their new office HQ. 30 Brock Street
will provide 20,000 sq ft of offices designed by Marshall Architects and Tate Hindle,
with 3,500 sq ft floorplates arranged over the first to sixth floors.

www.regentsplace.com

Founded: 1986

Shaftesbury PLC — Chinatown, Carnaby & Seven Dials

Although Shaftesbury is a company that is only 27 years old, it takes a long-term view of sustaining the prosperity and vibrancy of the West End. Unlike other estates it is a FTSE 350 public company, with a mainly institutional shareholder base, but has adopted a similar management approach based on the aim of providing a sustainable framework in which commercial tenants are able to flourish and where people want to live and work, and enjoy their leisure time.

Shaftesbury was formed in 1986 and listed on the London Stock Exchange in 1987. Since the early 1990s it has employed a consistent strategy of investing only in the heart of the West End, a location which has demonstrated great long-term resilience in tenant demand. This area is an international tourist destination with an estimated 200 million visits annually, including Londoners and UK visitors, and has a large working population (600,000 in the City of Westminster as a whole) in fashion, media, IT and creative industry sectors, as well as being one of the world's major shopping destinations. In addition it contains or is near to internationally renowned visitor attractions such as Buckingham Palace, and at its heart is London's unrivalled theatre district along with restaurants, galleries and cinemas. Much of Shaftesbury's portfolio is within five minutes' walk of two of the main interchanges for Crossrail, Tottenham Court Road and Bond Street.

The company originally owned property in Chinatown, but its wholly owned portfolio, valued in 2012 at £1.8 billion, now extends to 13 acres of freeholds across central London covering more than 1.6 million sq ft of commercial and residential space in over 500 buildings. It includes 330 shops and 230 restaurants, providing 70 per cent of overall income, 390,000 sq ft of offices and 500 flats offered on shorthold tenancies. The estate is characterised by properties with a mix of uses – a shop or restaurant on the lower floor and office or residential (or a combination of both) on the upper floor. Smaller offices tend to suffer from cyclical demand and obsolescence, but, with growing demand for residential accommodation in these central locations, many offices have been returned to their historic use as residential.

Around 20 per cent of properties are listed and all are within conservation areas, located in street patterns that were established 1680–1720 after building here proliferated west of the City after the Great Fire. Shaftesbury is also a partner in the Longmartin joint venture with the Mercers' Company (see page 27), which owns a 1.9 acre island site in Covent Garden providing 269,000 sq ft of mixed-use accommodation.

The policy for investment is to focus on areas where the company can become the main owner and to build up clusters of ownerships. This has enabled the creation of urban villages that can accommodate a variety of uses appealing to a broad range of occupiers. As long-term investors, the company takes a consistent approach to the management of its holdings through a holistic strategy which brings cohesion to streets and public spaces, and where a consistent level of quality in both public realm and the retail and leisure offer can be maintained. This approach focuses on the economic sustainability of its areas as well as improving the physical environment.

Each village has a different focus, with Shaftesbury pursuing a policy of creating a long-term tenant mix adapted to the prevailing features of the area and constantly changing consumer tastes, in order to create distinctive destinations. All these villages have their own brand, including promotion through events, dedicated websites and other media. Carnaby Street, synonymous with 1960s swinging London, seeks to reinforce its reputation as a centre for youth fashion and pop music culture, and hence trend-focused retailing is dominant, with independent boutiques positioned alongside major international flagship and concept stores. Holdings in Covent Garden, which are centred on Seven Dials, the Opera Quarter and Coliseum and the

Top: Chinatown
Above: Seven Dials

joint venture at St Martin's Courtyard (see page 28), provide a diverse retail, leisure and cultural offer for a slightly older demographic. Chinatown has a long-established reputation as a Far Eastern restaurant quarter with both a robust daytime and night-time economy: Hong Kong immigrants settled here after World War II when leases were short and rents were low owing to a planned large-scale redevelopment at the time. Shaftesbury also owns property in Soho, principally on and around Berwick Street, home to tailoring and textile stores and central London's largest concentration of independent vinyl record stores. Charlotte Street is the oldest restaurant street in the West End.

To continue to maintain the appeal of its holdings, the company researches potential new tenants from abroad and aims to bring in new retail and restaurant concepts. Like many other estates, the company has invested in the public realm to enhance the appeal of its villages, with pavements, street lighting and other servicing, and events, press partnerships and shopping evenings to bring in new trade. In the same way it has supported local charities and education initiatives, including bursaries for catering and fashion students at the nearby Kingsway College and London College of Fashion.

Below: St Martin's Courtyard

www.shaftesbury.co.uk

Founded: 1987

Canary Wharf and Wood Wharf

Since its creation two decades ago, Canary Wharf has become an established part of London's urban landscape. Its transformation from derelict dockland to international business, shopping and residential district is one of the most significant of any city in the world. The area on the Isle of Dogs covers more than 97 acres and about 15 million sq ft of office and retail space has been constructed to date, by some of the world's leading architects, with more than 105,000 people working on the estate and more locally as a result of its transformation of the area.

The London Docklands Development Corporation was established in 1980/81 and was tasked with regenerating the former docklands by bringing land and buildings back into use, encouraging industry and commerce, creating an attractive environment, and assisting in the provision of housing and social facilities. The development of Canary Wharf began with the decision by Credit Suisse First Boston to create a back office and with G Ware Trevelstead's plans to create a 10 million sq ft financial centre, a project taken over by Olympia & York with agreement to construct in 1987. The iconic One Canada Square, with its steel pyramid, was completed in 1990 and the first tenants moved in in 1991. The property market collapsed with the early 1990s and Olympia & York went into administration. It was subsequently bought in 1995 by an international consortium that later became Canary Wharf Group.

Currently the development comprises 35 completed buildings and more than 200 shops, bars and restaurants within four retail malls. It also has a conference and banqueting centre, Docklands Light Railway and Jubilee Line stations, car parks and approximately 20 acres of landscaped open spaces. Occupiers on the Canary Wharf estate include some of the world's leading business organisations from the media, legal, accounting, financial services, IT, energy and transport sectors.

Canary Wharf Group PLC, now owns, develops, constructs and manages property in Canary Wharf, as an integrated group of companies. As of 2012 the market value of the Group's investment property portfolio, including land, was £5.2 billion, and the average unexpired lease length was 16 years.

Its subsidiary, Canary Wharf Management Limited, manages all of the external areas on what remains a privately owned estate, and management services are also provided for occupiers. In line with the original intention to provide an attractive environment, 20 per cent of external spaces are landscaped parks, plazas and walkways. A programme of more than 100 arts and cultural events every year also seeks to enhance the spaces open to the public. Canary Wharf Contractors manages the design and construction of all the buildings, retail malls and infrastructure on the estate, and of the Group's projects in other parts of the city, including the Shell Centre on the South Bank, a joint venture with Qatari Diar and 20 Fenchurch Street in the City of London, with Land Securities.

Over the next 20 years the intention is to double the working population of Canary Wharf which reflects too the rapid changes that have seen the expansion of East London, not only with the regeneration for the 2012 Olympic and Paralympic Games but also the expansion of infrastructure, and in particular the DLR, Jubilee and East London lines, and the development of surrounding areas such as Deptford and the Royal Docks.

Wood Wharf, a 20-acre site in the north-east of the Isle of Dogs next to Canary Wharf, is part of the next step to ensure that, like the other estates, Canary Wharf continues a dynamic development philosophy to ensure the long-term prosperity for it and the surrounding area by continuing to provide what the market needs. Wood Wharf was once used as an area for the shipping and storage of timber and the repair of ships, and its development is designed to increase the size of the overall

estate by a third. It is intended to be truly mixed-use sustainable community with a range of homes, offices, shops and community facilities, set within a water space and public realm. The development is designed to create approximately 25,000 new jobs, more than 3,000 new homes and a significant retail provision within an energetic public realm.

An original masterplan was created by Rogers Stirk Harbour and Partners and submitted for planning in 2008, with consent granted in 2009. In 2012 Canary Wharf Group bought the Wood Wharf site from its previous development partners and engaged Terry Farrell and Partners in a new design exercise to develop a strategy for the site in view of the changed global economic situation. The new masterplan focused development towards residential and the TMT (technology, media and telecommunications) industry sector. This plan has now been developed into the current strategy by Allies and Morrison, appointed in early 2013, with Sir Terry Farrell continuing to provide design advice as the scheme progresses. Following extensive consultation with residents, businesses, community groups and wider stakeholders since August 2012, the scheme is expected to be submitted for planning approval in late 2013.

Growth sectors such as technology and new media generally require smaller and more flexible office space rather than the larger trading floors associated with the financial sector. The aim is thus to offer more flexible accommodation into

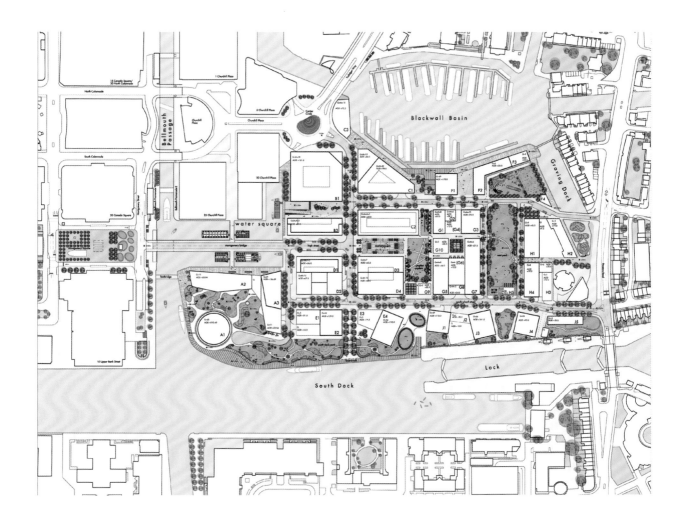

Above: Indicative
masterplan for
Wood Wharf
Allies and Morrison,
September 2013

which smaller firms can move quickly and adapt easily for new uses. This approach
is already being implemented at Canary Wharf itself, with selective transition
from single occupancy to multi-tenanted buildings, where parts of existing floors
can be adapted for new start-ups on shorter leases, including hot desking, shared
and co-working spaces for creative industry and TMT companies. This again is a
prime example of how estates try to respond to changing market forces by adapting
properties designed for one purpose into another.

Similarly, Wood Wharf is attempting to create a community that will grow
organically and integrate more seamlessly into the wider urban and social fabric.
It will include a large amount of housing, including affordable and keyworker
housing, as well as all the features of a traditional estate – schools and healthcare
facilities, library and community buildings, and usable green space. In particular it
seeks to create a new destination for local people including the working population
of Canary Wharf, local residents and surrounding businesses as well as new
employees and residents, and by having land under one ownership – as was always
a feature in the original estates – a more robust and clear planning and development
process can take place.

www.canarywharf.com; www.woodwharf.com

Founded: 1999

More London

More London is a 13.5-acre mixed-use business estate on the south bank of the Thames between London Bridge and Tower Bridge, now wholly owned by London Bridge Holdings and managed by More London Estates. Masterplan led by Foster + Partners, it is home to City Hall, housing the chamber for the London Assembly and the offices of the Mayor and staff of the Greater London Authority, and 12 further buildings. These provide a diverse mix of grade A office space, shops, restaurants, bars, a hotel, a theatre, and a unique open-air music and entertainment amphitheatre. The site occupies a key strategic location on the Thames riverside, and hence over the last decade has provided a significant driver for regeneration in the London Borough of Southwark.

Before its current incarnation, the site was part of Hay's Wharf, which extended from London Bridge to Tower Bridge and was located within the area known as the Pool of London. The area became known as London's Larder owing to the vast range of food such spices, tea, coffee and cocoa traded and stored here. With the introduction of containerisation the docks moved further east, and the warehouses fell into dereliction. In 1983 approval was given for a primarily commercial scheme, but the site remained closed until permission for what is now More London was granted to More London Development in 1999, with construction beginning in 2000. 7 More London Riverside, the final and largest building, was completed in 2010.

Below: More London, viewed from the Thames' north bank

The estate now has a working community of about 20,000 people, with approximately 90 per cent of the space occupied by offices. Most of these are single lets on leases of 25 years or more to large corporates in accountancy and law, in particular EY, PwC and Norton Rose Fulbright, as well as finance and advertising. Key to all estates, however, is the recognition that the area provides facilities beyond just a single use and More London was always envisioned not just as a place to work. Investment in and careful management of the public spaces and on-site managed facilities and amenities have ensured that it has also become a vibrant destination attracting 10 million visitors a year.

The Scoop at More London is a 1,000-seat sunken amphitheatre providing year round exhibitions and a summer festival programme of theatre, music, film and art. Again this shows how estates are seeking to retain and renew interest by providing a much broader and creative approach to placemaking than just managed office spaces.

Core to the original masterplan was a diagonal boulevard from Tooley Street, with the Tower of London a visual focal point at the end. The area is intersected by smaller routes and alleyways with water features, trees and street furniture integrated into the overall hard landscaping. Public realm improvements in and near the area have included new riverside lighting and the creation of Potters Field Park providing public green spaces. A unique feature is the common serviced subterranean roadway that takes vehicles off the street and away from pedestrians.

www.morelondon.com

Founded: 2002
Acquired by Qatari Diar
Delancey in 2011

East Village London

The East Village, next to the Queen Elizabeth Olympic Park, is London's newest neighbourhood. In its physical aspects, layout and management it has been influenced heavily by the model of the original great estates, with the aim of creating a new mixed, integrated community for the 21st century – a place where people will stay, with not only high-quality homes but also education and healthcare facilities, outdoor space, local shops and community facilities.

The new neighbourhood will initially deliver nearly 3,000 new homes from the end of 2013. There will be over 1,400 private homes available to rent, which will be owned and managed by Get Living London, a company set up by Qatari Diar Delancey (a joint venture between Qatari Diar Real Estate Development Company and Delancey). There will also be 1,379 affordable homes owned by Triathlon Homes, comprising 675 social rent homes, 356 intermediate rent homes, and 348 homes available through shared ownership.

East Village was the Athletes' Village during the 2012 Olympic and Paralympic Games, but was actually part of a masterplan that had been conceived for the Stratford City development submitted for planning in 2002, well before the success of London's bid for the Games was announced in 2005. The 27-hectare site was part of a scheme to regenerate a neglected part of east London, transforming derelict railway land into a new district complete with shopping centre (now Westfield), offices and homes. The designs were developed in 1997 by Stanhope and Chelsfield. After a bid for the Games was announced, the government – in the form of the Olympic Delivery Authority (ODA) – became developer of the Park and the Village, with Lend Lease acting as project manager on the housing.

Planning permission was granted in 2005, and in 2007 the ODA, in conjunction with the Architecture Foundation, issued an international call for architects to design the Village; 16 leading practices were chosen. Construction began in 2008 and in 2011 it was announced that the private housing element, along with six adjacent development plots for a potential 2,000 further homes in the future, had been sold to Qatari Diar Delancey. The joint-venture invested more than £500 million in the purchase and long-term management of the Village, including arrangements to provide a future profit share for the public sector.

The neighbourhood, masterplanned by Fletcher Priest, is arranged in 11 residential plots, each mostly comprising six or seven blocks built around a central landscaped courtyard. The blocks in each plot have been designed by two or three firms of architects and range from eight to twelve storeys with three-storey town houses at street level. Most benefit from a dual aspect with views at the front and into the courtyard. Most also have balconies, some have winter gardens and all town houses have private terraces. Together with the courtyard areas which provide residents with landscaped gardens and children's play areas, the East Village site also provides more than 10 hectares of new parks and public open space, including more than 2,500 trees.

The form and layout was inspired by those of the London estates, in particular the sizes of streets and open spaces, and the mansion block typologies, of Marylebone, and by the configuration of shared amenity spaces in relation to private dwellings in other established areas in London.

East Village is the first development of this scale to achieve Level 4 of the Code for Sustainable Homes. Rainwater harvesting is used to water communal landscapes and gardens. All energy is produced locally through Combined Cooling Heat and Power (CCHP) Plants which reduces carbon emissions by 68 per cent compared to similar residential developments.

In the same way that the original estates were self-contained, incorporating all

Above: East Village
Right: View out to the City
and beyond

the services that residents required, East Village will provide a wide range of facilities for new residents. There will be educational facilities in the form of Chobham Academy, for 1,800 students aged between 3 and 19 years, GP services and a pharmacy at the Sir Ludwig Guttman Medical Centre.

Shopping facilities are provided nearby in the form of Westfield Stratford City, and Get Living London will also be creating a new neighbourhood retail offer. The retail space on the Village estate – about 34 shops – will include a gym and provide quality services, shops, cafes and restaurants. The retail tenants will be a mix of local, multiple and independent operators let on a variety of lease terms with the shops to be launched in spring 2014. The retail offer will be supported by an enlivenment and community programme where initiatives will include support for local clubs and societies, weekly markets, an annual fete, and an arts and culture programme to build up opportunities for social interaction between residents.

East Village is adjacent to the Queen Elizabeth Olympic Park with 252 acres of parkland, waterways and trails – as well as leisure facilities including the Aquatics Centre and Velodrome. In addition Stratford International and Stratford Regional Station provides connections to central London and the continent via Eurostar.

All of Get Living London's 1,439 private homes will be available on a rental-only basis and let directly to residents, without middlemen managers or agents. Equally innovative for new schemes in London are options for private rental tenancy agreements of up to three years, with flexibility and resident-only break clauses, to encourage people to stay longer within the community.

To further encourage long-term occupation, East Village's approach follows traditional long-term estate management – a dedicated company, East Village Management, has been set up to own all buildings, communal areas and public realm, and to ensure they are continually maintained to high standards. Another aspect in common with many other great estates is the 'hands-on' and robust approach to relations between landlord and resident through the provision of an on-site Management Centre, with a dedicated team available to respond to residents' needs.

www.eastvillagelondon.co.uk

Right: Courtyard modelled on original London squares
Below: Landscaping within East Village

Founded: 2006

Covent Garden

Since 2006 Capital & Counties Properties PLC ('Capco') has been transforming Covent Garden with the aim of re-establishing it as a globally renowned retail, leisure and residential district through a combination of asset management, strategic investment and development. The estate now encompasses 900,000 sq ft of mixed-use space and includes 63 properties, with a value of £1.1 billion, and represents 55 per cent of Capco's gross assets.

Part of Capco's strategy in restoring the area's vibrancy has been to draw on, highlight and maintain Covent Garden's distinctive cultural, architectural and economic heritage. The area covered by the Covent Garden estate – broadly bordered by Long Acre, Bedford Street, Maiden Lane, Tavistock Street and Bow Street – was largely pasture that once belonged to the Abbey (or Convent) of St Peter at Westminster. Much of this 'Convent Garden' land was granted to John Russell, 1st Earl of Bedford (see Bedford Estates, page 45), after the Dissolution of the Monasteries in the 1540s.

In 1630 Francis Russell, 4th Earl of Bedford, commissioned the architect Inigo Jones to build houses on the site that would be 'fit for the habitations of gentlemen and men of ability'. The result was a revolutionary development in town planning in England: a new square, or piazza, modelled on the Renaissance architecture that Jones had seen on his visit to Italy. It was surrounded on one side by St Paul's Church, which still stands, and on the other three by rows of tall terraced houses with gardens, coach houses and stabling that were soon attracting rich and fashionable tenants.

In 1670 the Earl and his heirs were granted by royal charter the right to hold a market for flowers, fruit and vegetables which grew rapidly in size and popularity. By the mid-18th century the well-to-do residents began to move west to fashionable new developments in Soho and Mayfair, and the area became popular with actors and artists, and many theatres including the Theatre Royal on Drury Lane were built, as well as the Royal Opera House.

Owing to rapid and unregulated growth of the fruit and vegetable market, the 6th Duke of Bedford commissioned architect Charles Fowler to build the neo-classical Market Building in 1828. Ownership of the market passed from the Bedford family to the Covent Garden Estate Company in 1918, and, as the fruit and vegetable market continued to grow, in 1974 it moved to new premises at Nine Elms.

The market traders moved out and the site was acquired by the Greater London Council (GLC) but fell into disrepair. Many buildings were listed after public protest at plans for redevelopment and in 1975 the GLC began major restoration work on the central Market Building, which opened as Europe's first speciality shopping centre. In 1988 the Covent Garden Area Trust was set up to ensure that the area's unique character would be preserved. Every year the Trust pays annual rent of one red apple and a posy of flowers as part of its 150-year lease of the Market Building.

Capco purchased the Covent Garden estate in 2006 and began to revitalise the area through an approach founded on the model of the great estates. One of the key aims was to change perceptions of the area from a mass-market tourist destination to one for discerning urban audiences. Like many other estates, the area is mixed-use and Capco has enhanced the area's unique retail and food offer, attracting 44 million customer visitors per year. Since the original purchase, Capco has continued to grow the estate through tactical acquisitions to expand the portfolio, while reinvesting and improving the fabric of the historic buildings and public realm, resulting in significantly increased value and an improved visitor experience.

Under Capco's stewardship more than 60 new brands have opened for business. These are a combination of larger, global names such as Apple, Burberry, Chanel

Below: Covent Garden

and Dior, as well as smaller, emerging brands like fashion emporium Opening Ceremony. New openings include Australian beauty brand Aesop, French fashion label Sandro and luxury sportswear concept Y-3. Short leases outside the 1954 Act ensure curatorial control can be maintained by Capco and brands can flex and grow in the space as needed. Capco has sought to further the estate's reputation as a gourmet food destination by bringing in new restaurants such as the first London branch of Manhattan's Balthazar and Balthazar Boulangerie, American burger phenomenon Shake Shack, Parisian patisserie Ladurée and Danish-Japanese concept Sticks 'n Sushi. Visitor interest is further stimulated through temporary uses and pop-ups as well as a comprehensive programme of cultural events curated and delivered by Capco's in-house team.

The reintroduction of luxury residential has connected Covent Garden with its residential roots. The Henrietta and The Russell have set new standards for quality and pricing in the area. The Beecham and The Southampton are both set to come to market in 2014 along with a raft of rental properties.

Like many estates, the quality of public space is a key priority in the strategy for Covent Garden. The area is characterised by distinctive narrow streets, especially north of the Piazza, and small alleyways and passages which encourage visitors to 'discover' new spaces. A new mixed-use development is proposed between Floral Street and King Street known as Kings Court and Carriage Hall, which will involve the creation of a new retail passage connecting Long Acre and King Street. This aims to improve pedestrian movement in the district and open the existing courtyard area to the public. High quality new residential space will occupy the upper levels with views over the courtyard and retail and restaurant space on the ground level.

www.coventgardenlondonuk.com

Below: Floral Arcade with restored market building to the left
Right: Covent Garden Market, Charles Fowler, 1828, view from south east

Founded: 2006

Victoria

Land Securities is in the process of creating a new commercial, retail and residential heart for Victoria, where, as the major landowner, it has initiated a £2 billion programme of investment to transform the area over the coming decade.

Victoria is one of the most visited parts of London, and has one of the capital's major transport hubs through which 150 million passengers pass every year. Despite this, until recently most of its office space was outdated and the public realm unattractive. Land Securities' plan aims to deliver better pedestrianised routes as well as, through redevelopment and refurbishment, a more varied streetscape of office, retail and residential space to create a place in which people want to work, shop, live and socialise. The work began in 2006 with the completion of the retail/office development Cardinal Place, designed by EPR Architects.

Since then development and refurbishment has continued with Wellington House, completed in 2012, a mixed-use building with retail on the ground floor and 59 luxury apartments above; 62 Buckingham Gate, a landmark prism-like structure for office and retail, designed by Pelli Clarke Pelli / Swanke Hayden Connell and completed in 2013; and 123 Victoria Street, a 227,230 sq ft development of repositioned office space and shops designed by Wilkinson Eyre and Auckett Fitzroy Robinson, completed in 2012. Occupiers include the luxury fashion brand Jimmy Choo.

Projects underway include Kings Gate, a 12-storey residential building comprising 100 apartments, and the Zig Zag Building, a 190,000 sq ft office building over 14 floors. Both are due for completion in 2015 and will provide a new and enhanced retail offer, together with considerable improvements to the public realm benefiting the wider Victoria area. The development also provides for an affordable housing contribution of £11.6 million. Victoria Circle (Nova) will lead to a vast increase in public space across an 81,800 sqm site around Victoria Station and includes space for a new public library. Phased completion is expected between 2016 and 2018.

http://createvictoria.com/

Right: Aerial photograph of Victoria Street showing recent developments and projects

Founded: 2008

King's Cross

The new urban quarter emerging at King's Cross under the ownership of the King's Cross Central Limited Partnership is one that has drawn strongly on the precedents of urban planning and management developed by the great historic estates, while reinterpreting them for contemporary requirements. In common with other estates, the development seeks to optimise the value of the assets, socially as well as economically, and takes the approach that by enhancing the quality of life long-term value and resilience can be created.

In the 18th century King's Cross was a small village named Battle Bridge, but also the site of St Chad's Well, a spa attracting 800-900 people every day; in 1836 the name of the area was changed to King's Cross after a statue of George IV was erected here (which provoked such disparaging comment that it was taken down in 1842). In the 1850s the Great Northern Railway built its London terminus, designed by Lewis Cubitt, here, which at the time was the largest station in England. The area then developed as an industrial heartland, which a century later had become derelict, largely owing to the decline in the transport of freight by rail.

The 1996 decision to move the Channel Tunnel Rail Link from Waterloo to St Pancras resulted in the then principal landowners – London & Continental Railways Limited and Excel (now DHL) resolving to develop the land, and Argent was selected as the developer in 2000, with Allies and Morrison and Porphyrios Associates as masterplanners. In 2008, Argent, London & Continental Railways and DHL formed a joint venture, King's Cross Central Limited Partnership, which is now the single landowner. Argent is also the asset manager.

The aim is to establish a 'whole new piece' of London, with 2,000 homes,

Below: Building B2 overlooking King's Cross St Pancras station, David Chipperfield Architects

3.4 million sq ft of workspace, and 500,000 sq ft of retail, for 45,000 people, over a 67 acre site. A focus on public realm is a priority – there will be 26 acres of public space and 10 new public squares. Initial phases of development have been directed towards establishing key public realm and key infrastructure such as roads, bridges and utilities, on which some £300 million of initial investment has been spent. The new quarter is now taking shape with the opening of the University of the Arts London, Granary Square, King's Bridge and King's Boulevard.

Ten key principles were used in formulating the masterplan for King's Cross, of which probably three are directly drawn from the great estates model or similar to their philosophy – creating a robust urban framework, committing to long-term success and making a lasting new place.

Defining the masterplan was core to the development of this site over 67 acres. The team looked at many historical precedents including the great London estates and parts of the West End, Soho, Marylebone and the City fringes to identify how to lay out new streets and squares, and how to create 'delight and surprise'. It is the durability of this physical framework, it is argued, that is fundamental to the creation of successful places – the buildings are important, but they come and go over time. This framework also addresses the effective integration of the parts into a whole and its connections with pre-existing neighbouring urban spaces. Alongside this the masterplan and individual buildings were also intended to accommodate change over time, to ensure their lasting ecomomic, cultural and environmental value.

To deliver a viable mixed-use urban quarter, good stewardship over the long-term was also seen as vital. The joint venture established an ownership structure for the development that ensures that it can be managed proactively as a whole. The public areas and many of the buildings are managed and maintained by a specialist on-site team – King's Cross Estate Services – which, as well as keeping the area well-maintained, well-lit, safe and secure, is also involved in organising and managing events and activities and working with the local community and local authorities.

The team looked, for example, at how to create a viable mix, exploring questions such as how many different types of use are actually needed to create overall a mixed-use feel. Control over estate management including such aspects as signage is also in place even for those properties where the long-term interest has been given away.

The aim was to create a series of places with a relationship that can adapt over time: the masterplan creates a public realm that binds the place together, as occupiers take over organically. Ultimately King's Cross itself may become a series of distinct places. It will have different associations for different people rather than one identity, creating a series of world-class destinations and places.

www.kingscross.co.uk

Top right: Google HQ at King's Cross, view from Granary Square, AHMM
Far right: Granary Square, Regent's Canal seating

Founded: 2009

Earls Court

The vision for this new neighbourhood in west London, currently under development by Capco and joint venture partners, takes the story of London's estates into the mid-21st century and beyond, by applying the enduring principles of high-density patterns of streets, squares and mansion blocks that have characterised the capital over the past 400 years. The creation of London's newest great estate seeks to provide 7,500 homes under the auspices of Sir Terry Farrell's vision of 'four new urban villages and a high street' which would be an integral part of the existing urban landscape where Kensington, Chelsea and Fulham meet.

Earls Court derives its name from the courthouse of the Earls of Warwick and Holland, who were once lords of the manor, and was originally a series of hamlets in Middlesex, around the 'lost river' of Counter's Creek. The area became synonymous with market gardens, but large-scale development began in the 19th century. Counter's Creek was converted first into the Kensington Canal in the 1820s, then filled in to create the West London Extension Railway in 1863. The Metropolitan Railway was built in the 1860s, and terraced houses were built for railway workers and clerks.

The tradition of entertainment in Earls Court began in 1887, when the entrepreneur John Robinson Whitley opened an entertainment ground on derelict land between two railway lines. This spectacular covered space had gardens, rides, pavilions and a grand arena where he staged Buffalo Bill's Wild West Show. Whitley also built the famous Earls Court Gigantic Wheel, with impressive views over London. The current Earls Court Exhibition Halls were built in the 1930s and were the largest reinforced concrete building in Europe at the time, covering 12 acres. In recent years the surrounding area has undergone a renaissance, with the old power station on Lots Road being redeveloped, White City transforming into a vast new shopping complex and Old Oak Common chosen as a prime site for a high-speed super rail station connecting Heathrow with the rest of Britain.

The Earls Court Project began in 2009 with a Collaboration Agreement between the three project partners – Capco, the London Borough of Hammersmith & Fulham (LBHF), and Transport for London (TfL) – to pursue a strategic approach that sought benefits for the whole area. Terry Farrell and Partners was appointed to develop the masterplan after winning an international competition in 2010.

The Earls Court and West Kensington Opportunity Area (ECWKOA), recognised by the Mayor's London Plan in 2011, covers 77 acres across the boundaries of the boroughs of the London Borough of Hammersmith & Fulham and the Royal Borough of Kensington & Chelsea (RBKC). Its borders run along Warwick Road to the east, Lillie Road to the south, North End Road to the west and West Cromwell Road (the A4) to the north. The ECWKOA comprises three main areas of land: the Earls Court Exhibition Centre (owned by Capco) and its car park on Seagrave Road (owned by Capco and KFI), the West Kensington and Gibbs Green housing estates (owned by LBHF), and the Lillie Bridge rail depot (owned by TfL). Resolution to grant planning permission was achieved by LBHF and RBKC in autumn 2012 and formal planning consent is due to be granted shortly on completion of the Section 106 agreement. Lillie Square, the residential scheme on Seagrave Road which will transform the Earls Court Exhibition Centre car park into 808 new homes set around outstanding communal gardens, received formal planning consent from LBHF in March 2012 and construction on site is expected to start during 2013.

The redevelopment of Earls Court will be a long-term project and it is envisaged that it will be delivered in seven phases. The four urban villages – Earls Court, North End, West Kensington and West Brompton – will include not only homes but

Top right: Earls Court Village, Farrells
Far right: Earls Court, Farrells

also retail and restaurant spaces, hotels, work space, a hospital and education and community facilities. The masterplan's hierarchy of uses and movement will echo historic districts such as Mayfair and the streetscapes will evolve and knit organically over time into those of the existing surrounding neighbourhoods. A new high street will make a dramatic difference to the accessibility and draw of the Earls Court area, and a new London park will weave through the heart of the scheme offering a variety of leisure uses and a range of hard and soft landscaping.

The next decade will see the vision for Earls Court emerge in detail. The first buildings and green spaces of the new district will be seen in Lillie Square and the south-east corner of the scheme. A series of 'meanwhile activities' will animate and stimulate the area during the construction phases and form the foundations for the creation of a strong sense of place for this new great London estate.

www.myearlscourt.com

Below: Visualisation of
new high street

Founded: 2012

Queen Elizabeth Olympic Park

The London Legacy Development Corporation (LLDC) is a Mayoral Development Corporation, a public-sector, not-for-profit organisation, that is responsible for the long-term planning, development, management and maintenance of the Queen Elizabeth Olympic Park (QEOP) and its facilities after the London 2012 Olympic and Paralympic Games, including the creation of five new neighbourhoods. LLDC's stated purpose is to "promote and deliver physical, social, economic and environmental regeneration of the Olympic Park and its surrounding area". It is also the planning authority for the area under its remit.

In line with the existing great estates, LLDC intends on using its freehold ownership to positively promote design and management quality standards, in order to sustain long-term value in the physical aspects of the QEOP Estate, and reinvest revenues in the further improvement and management of the Park. The physical regeneration of this part of east London was one of the most important legacy promises of the original London bid for the Games. After the Games, the immediate priority was the transformation of the Olympic site into the legacy Park through a £300 million construction project that involved removing temporary venues, turning permanent venues into everyday use, building new roads and bridges, building visitor centres and landscape play and recreational areas. The overall strategy is designed to deliver five new neighbourhoods in Hackney Wick, Leyton, Stratford, Fish Island and Pudding Mill, with up to 8,000 new homes in addition to the 2,800 in the former Athletes' Village (now East Village; see page 104), along with schools, nurseries, health centres, playgrounds, local greens and convenience retail. These are strategically positioned on the edges of QEOP to ensure strong connections between the existing and new neighbourhoods. Detailed plans for the first neighbourhood, Chobham Manor, are well underway. There will also be 22 miles of pathways, waterways and cycle paths and 252 acres of open space, and in terms of infrastructure, direct connections to a third of London's rail and underground lines.

Below: The evolving estate

Many aspects of the project are modelled explicitly on the great estates of central London. It is a large-scale, mixed-use site currently under single ownership – with a responsibility to repay capital receipts from disposals to government but also maintain a revenue line to help fund the ongoing management and maintenance of the Park and all its venue facilities, events and community activities. Thus by retaining its freehold interest LLDC retains direct control over the long-term vision for the sustainable growth of this new piece of city.

Attention to design quality at all levels – both at the urban and the architectural scale – has the ultimate aim of providing a greater sense of place and thus supporting the creation of a new piece of city. The urban blocks so familiar from the traditional great estates have been translated into contemporary forms for the Legacy Communities Scheme (LLDC's masterplan) that accommodate houses with gardens, flats, maisonettes in three- to five-storey buildings framing main streets and waterways.

Three of the five neighbourhoods in the Park are reinterpretations of traditional London housing, designed to provide the desperately needed family housing that will reverse the transient population trend in this part of London. In the same way that housebuilding in the 18th and 19th centuries was stimulated by neighbouring

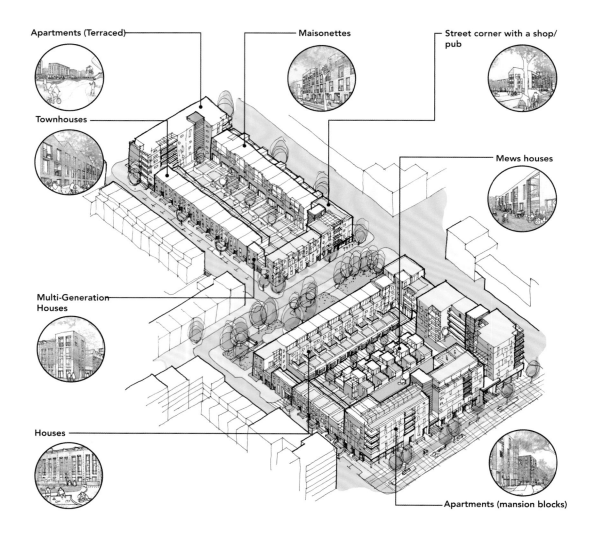

Apartments (Terraced)

Townhouses

Multi-Generation Houses

Houses

Maisonettes

Street corner with a shop/pub

Mews houses

Apartments (mansion blocks)

Left: Chobham typologies, PRP
Above: Stratford Waterfront

developments, so these new neighbourhoods will be orientated towards existing ones, and there will be local public spaces as well as the wider park.

As the major landowner in the Park, the Legacy Corporation will retain ultimate responsibility for management and maintenance of public parkland and venue facilities including the Aquatics Centre, Copper Box and ArcelorMittal Orbit. Alongside LLDC's grant funding from the GLA, estate revenue income will comprise occupational rents, profit rent and other revenues from events, attractions, sponsorship and advertising within the Park Estate, as well as a fixed Estate Charge to be paid by residential and commercial occupiers of the Development Zones as a contribution towards the Estate Services.

LLDC will dispose of Development Zones to developers via long leaseholds with individual properties then being sold with obligations relating to design and management quality standards and the payment of a fixed Estate Charge. To reduce the risk of leasehold enfranchisement legislation undermining the estate strategy, houses will be sold freehold via a direct transfer from LLDC to the house purchaser and apartments sold leasehold via a long lease granted by the developer.

This approach has been influenced by the principles and lessons learned from the great estates, in emphasising the importance of a long-term vision to protect common amenities and maintain a high-quality environment. The Legacy Corporation is also exploring opportunities for higher education and cultural institutions relocating to the Park to help establish the destination. The Legacy Corporation will also provide a range of events in venues and open spaces in the Park, including concerts, exhibitions, markets and carnivals in the South Park and smaller-scale community events in the more pastoral settings of the North Park.

In creating five new communities LLDC is generating a sustainable long-term income via long leasehold disposals of land to ensure it will eventually become a self-sufficient entity. In addition to this LLDC is also exploring the creation of longer-term structures which will survive after it has ceased to exist, in order to deliver the objectives for this part of London.

www.londonlegacy.co.uk

Founded: 2013

Paddington Central

In July 2013 British Land acquired assets comprising the majority of Paddington Central, a 1.2 million sq ft office-led, mixed-use estate close to Paddington station. The acquisition was in line with British Land's strategy of increasing its office portfolio in the West End, and its well-established approach in managing and developing major office-led estates through its ownership of Broadgate (see page 90) and Regent's Place (see page 93) will be applied here. Opportunities include letting the remaining vacant space, improving the public spaces, retail and leisure provision, and developing the sites to complete the estate.

Paddington Central is well positioned in terms of its proximity to Paddington Station, which will benefit both from the opening of the new Hammersmith & City

Right: Sheldon Square

line in 2014 and Crossrail in 2018, and rail connections to Heathrow Airport. The total estate comprises eight separate modern buildings, providing offices, a hotel, retail units and a health centre, as well as 200 residential units. British Land owns six of the eight existing buildings together with two of the development sites, which have planning consent for 355,000 sq ft of offices, and an area below the development sites, currently used by Crossrail, which will revert to British Land ownership by 2018 and provides 80,000 sq ft of further potential mixed-use development. On completion of the developments, the estate will grow to 1.6 million sq ft – British Land will own just over 1 million sq ft.

www.paddingtoncentrallondon.com

PROJECT SHOWCASE

The following pages present a variety of projects being delivered by NLA Partners for Great Estates across the capital. They are divided by type, representing the diversity of activity currently taking place.

COMMERCIAL

26-27 AYBROOK STREET W1U 4AN

The Aybrook Street project is located within the Harley Street Conservation Area. The extensively remodelled and refurbished building has realised the opportunity to bring the former vacant Police Station into viable office use, maximising its footprint by infilling to the Western building line with a new structure, extending floorplates and maximising the available light via generous West glazing. The building is entered from Aybrook Street either by the retained "barn door" historic driveway entrance or via a newly configured central entrance area with full disabled access. A new zinc clad mansard roof with dormer windows has been provided at roof level, opening onto some generous terrace spaces to the rear, which sit within the canopy of the magnificent London Plane trees.

Estate: The Howard de Walden Estate
Status: Completed in October 2008
Architect: ESA Design
Services engineer: Long & Partners
Structural engineer: Whitby Bird
Project manager: KHK

4 BENTINCK STREET (NOW NAMED HERON HOUSE) MARYLEBONE, W1U

This project presented an opportunity to demolish a 1960s building spanning plots 3-4 Bentinck Street and extending to Bentinck Mews behind. The new front facade plays with traditional architectural responses to context whilst employing contemporary detailing. The floorplates beyond and through to the mews side are expansive and efficient, and bathed in light from a lightwell to the east and substantially glazed internal elevations to a second floor mid-deck, hosting a green roof. A high BREEAM 'Very Good' was achieved, and sustainable energy sources stretched to provide a ground source heat pump system which linked 30 loop-in-piles with three 135m closed loop boreholes.

Estate: The Howard de Walden Estate
Status: Completed October 2009
Architect: ESA architecture/design
Service engineer: Long and Partners
Structural engineer: Buro Happold
Main contractor: Shepherd Construction
Project management: ESPM

65 DAVIES STREET W1

The 65,000 sq ft development will be located above the western ticket hall for Crossrail's new Bond Street station. The proposed scheme comprises of six floors of prime Mayfair office accommodation above the station, served by an entrance lobby on Davies Street. The contemporary office scheme has been carefully designed by PLP Architecture to be sensitive to the traditional architecture of neighbouring Mayfair buildings, incorporating high-quality natural materials with a detailed facade. The design incorporates a ventilation shaft that will be constructed as part of the works to build the Crossrail station western ticket hall.

Estate: The Grosvenor Estate
Status: Design stage, due to complete in 2019
Developer: Grosvenor and Crossrail
Architect: PLP
Structural & M&E engineer: Arup
Planning consultant: Gerald Eve
Project manager: Grosvenor
Cost consultant: E C Harris
Contractor: Sir Robert McAlpine

GOOGLE UK KING'S BOULEVARD, LONDON N1C

This innovative building designed by Allford Hall Monaghan Morris Architects will provide a dynamic and flexible working environment for up to 4,500 Google employees. Google has long-held aspirations to house all London-based staff under one roof and King's Cross was identified as an ideal place to locate the office. The building runs the length of King's Boulevard, from the new King's Cross concourse entrance to Goods Way, ranging in height from seven storeys at the station to 11 storeys at Goods Way. There will be shops and cafés at street level along King's Boulevard.

Estate: King's Cross (King's Cross Central Limited Partnership)
Status: Outline planning consent, reserved matters submitted
Architect: AHMM
Structural engineer: Waterman
M&E engineer: Hilson Moran
Planning consultant: Argent
Project manager: King's Cross Central Limited Partnership
Cost consultant: Davis Langdon (an AECOM company)

FIFTY GROSVENOR HILL W1K

Located in a discreet location in the heart of Mayfair, Fifty Grosvenor Hill is a 20,000 square feet multi-tenanted, BREEAM excellent, Grade A office building. The new development offers a historic mews facade design, a discreet and classic reception and contemporary interiors designed to the highest standard. Key features include exposed concrete soffit, chilled beams, raised flooring with 450mm void overall and displacement fresh air, bicycle storage with WCs, showers and lockers; and three self contained entrances leading to either Grosvenor Hill or Bourdon Street. Extensive public realm improvements surrounding the building incorporate public art sculptures of Terence Donovan and Twiggy by Neal French.

Estate: The Grosvenor Estate
Status: Completed May 2012
Architect: GMW
Structural engineer: Ramboll
M&E engineer: Hoare Lee
Planning consultant: Gerald Eve
Project manager: Grosvenor
Cost consultant: Davis Langdon
Contractor: Sir Robert McAlpine

69 GROSVENOR STREET W1K

The redevelopment of 69 Grosvenor Street will create a highly specified and innovative 'Townhouse' office building in Mayfair. The building will meet the needs of prime West End office occupiers who seek a residential feel to their office, taking advantage of its period Georgian features and incorporating contemporary open plan offices. The building will offer flexibility in letting options, including let as a whole, as two separate buildings or by individual floor. Features include a front and rear reception with passenger lifts, VRF fan coil air conditioning, showers, bicycle storage and two green roofs and has achieved EPC 'B' Rating and BREEAM 'Excellent'.

Estate: The Grosvenor Estate
Status: Under construction, due to complete Autumn 2014
Architect: ESA Architecture/Design
Service & structural engineer: Ramboll UK
Main contractor: Sir Robert McAlpine
Cost consultant: EC Harris

11 HARLEY STREET W1G

This complex project is to convert an Edwardian Harley Street building and 1960s Mews House into a new home for Isokinetic, a sports injury rehabilitation centre wishing to add a new London address to their portfolio of seven centres in Italy. A full demolition of the mews house and subsequent 5m deep excavation of the rear courtyard will create four floors of medical consulting, a 36 square metre aqua therapy pool, and a multi-tiered gymnasium with both open and private physiotherapy treatment space. High levels of glazing are to be used to replicate the bright, spacious environments of the Italian centres that are considered so essential to fast patient rehabilitation. Visual connections between each of the five zones allow patients to see and understand their journey to recovery.

Estate: The Howard de Walden Estate
Status: Under construction, due to complete May 2014
Architect: Sonnemann Toon Architects
Structural engineer: Fairhurst GGA
M&E engineer: Vector Designs

LONDON WALL PLACE 1 & 2 LONDON WALL PLACE, EC2M

London Wall Place is a new development strategically located in the City of London featuring two different yet, complementary office buildings totaling 500,000 sq ft. Replacing a 1950s podium and vacant tower, these buildings are easily reconfigurable, designed to accommodate constantly changing tenant needs and future environmental challenges. 1 London Wall Place will feature outdoor terraces with striking views towards St. Paul's Cathedral and other City landmarks. 2 London Wall Place will be a 16-storey tower offering spectacular views across the City. Over half of the site is dedicated to open space, creating a new destination for the area and a vibrant public place with a strong local identity, providing extraordinary gardens that reveal the Roman ruins of London Wall.

Estate: The City of London Corporation
Status: Planning granted August 2011, due to complete Q1 2016
Developers: Brookfield/Oxford Properties
Architect: Make Architects
Structural engineer: WSP UK Limited
M&E engineer: Hurley Palmer Flatt
Planning consultant: DP9
Project manager and cost consultant: Gardiner & Theobald LLP

114 – 116 MARYLEBONE LANE W1U

Originally constructed in the 1920s for a tool manufacturing company, and subsequently home to the Cordon Bleu school of cookery, the building is being transformed into a desirable modern office building aimed at attracting new kinds of occupier to Marylebone Village. The intricate redesign creates open, free flowing spaces with efficient floor plates and increased floor area. Fine finishes such as Bird's Eye Maple wall paneling are used as a foil to exposed brick, steel and polished concrete, giving the building an industrial yet sophisticated feel. The front elevation will be restored to reflect the art deco composition of Forbes and Tate's original drawings dating from 1927.

Estate: The Howard de Walden Estate
Status: Under construction, due to complete November 2013
Architect: Morrow + Lorraine Architects
Structural engineer: Fairhurst GGA
M&E engineer: Studio Nine
Project manager: Leslie Clark
Cost consultant: Leslie Clark
Contractor: Cameron Black

TWO PANCRAS SQUARE N1C

This Grade A office building, designed by international architects Allies and Morrison, offers approximately 130,000 square feet over nine floors, with floors ranging from 13,000 to 16,000 square feet. The south facing gardens and terraces on the top floor and rooftop offer superb views across Central London. The street level will house premier retail. Goods and services for this building will be delivered below street level via a shared access route.

Estate: King's Cross (King's Cross Central Limited Partnership)
Status: Under construction, due to complete July 2014
Architect: Allies and Morrison
Structural engineer: AKT
M&E engineer: Grontmij
Planning consultant: Argent
Project manager: King's Cross Central Limited Partnership
Cost consultant: Gardiner and Theobald
Contractor: Bam

64-66 WIGMORE STREET W1U

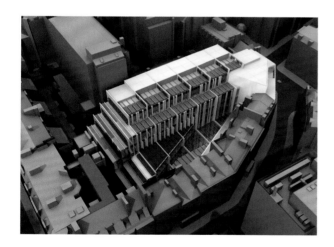

This project redevelops the site of a 1980s completed office building which was too onerous to adapt to current standards of accessibility. The new development maximises its site footprint and excavates to a further basement level with many technical challenges; a three-storey atrium occurs to the West, with further terracing-back occurring upwards from the first floor, creating green roof decks and following sunlight and daylight splays. High quality materials are to be used, with the Wigmore Street and Marylebone Lane facades displaying sensitively scaled designs fitting for the location but with contemporary detailing. The project is targeting a BREEAM rating of 'Excellent'.

Estate: The Howard de Walden Estate
Status: Under construction, due to complete September 2015
Architect: ESA architecture/design
Service engineer: Long & Partners
Structural engineer: WSP UK
Project management: ESPM
Cost consultant: Robinson Lowe Francis

80-81 WIMPOLE STREET W1

No 80 flanks the narrow roadway of Welbeck Way, and to the rear they abuts Margaret Howells fashion designer and the noise-sensitive Wigmore Hall with its classical receitals. Increasing development potential to the rear whilst respecting both overlooking concerns and sunlight/daylight splays was made possible by incorporating a staggered tier arrangement to the south with glazed roofs over a two-storey lightwell. Extensive temporary works were required within the shell to enable the new steel frame to be constructed within. The project achieved BREEAM 'Very Good'.

Estate: The Howard de Walden Estate
Status: Completed in October 2010
Architect: ESA Design
Services Engineer: RHB Partnership
Structural Engineer: Elliott Wood
Project Manager: ESPM

CENTRAL SAINT MARTINS / UNIVERSITY OF THE ARTS LONDON
THE GRANARY, N1C

The Granary and complex of new buildings, which once held Lincolnshire wheat for London's bakers, is now a creative warehouse for Central Saint Martins, part of University of the Arts London. These buildings have been designed by Stanton Williams Architects. Originally designed by Lewis Cubitt, the iconic building is the front door to the new university campus that extends 180 metres to the North, flanked on either side by the Transit Sheds. Internally, studios, workshops and lecture theatres are built around a broad, covered "street" with overhead walkways. The building also houses performance and exhibition spaces and the 350-seat Platform Theatre. The former stables now hold up to 275 bicycles.

Estate: King's Cross (King's Cross Central Limited Partnership)
Status: Completed in September 2011
Architect: Stanton Williams (with BAM Design and Weedon Partnership)
Structural engineer: Scott Willson (concept), BAM Design & Lister Beare (detail)
M&E engineer: Atelier Ten (concept), BAM Design (detail)
Planning consultant and project manager: Argent (acting on behalf of King's Cross Central Limited Partnership)
Cost consultant: Davis Langdon (an AECOM company)
Contractor: BAM Construction
Architectural lighting: Spiers & Major

THE LABORATORY, DULWICH COLLEGE DULWICH COMMON, SE21

Situated at the heart of the school's historic campus, adjacent to the Grade II* listed Charles Barry Jr building, Grimshaw's design for Dulwich College's new science building will replace an existing 1950s facility. The project was granted full planning approval in February 2013 and once complete it will be the first project to mark Dulwich College's 400th anniversary in 2019. The new building will provide state of the art new teaching accommodation in a continuous 'S' shape wrapped around two 'congregation' spaces which are linked into the surrounding landscaped grounds of the College.

Estate: The Dulwich Estate
Status: On site, due to complete in 2015
Client: Dulwich College
Architect & lead consultant: Grimshaw
Structural engineer: Alan Baxter Associates
M&E engineer: Mott MacDonald Fulcrum
Project manager: Blue Sky Building
Landscape: Land Use Consultants

HOTEL

GREAT NORTHERN HOTEL PANCRAS ROAD, N1C

The Great Northern Hotel first opened its doors in 1854 to the patrons of the Great Northern Railway Company, who made the hotel a glamorous destination and a stylish point of departure. Derelict for the past 12 years, the hotel has been brought back to life. The building, originally designed by Lewis Cubitt, has been exquisitely refurbished. The restoration has seen many of the hotel's original features retained and the redesign reflects all the style and class of this iconic building's past. There are over ninety luxurious rooms and broad corridors and wrought iron staircases sweep over the six floors.

Estate: King's Cross (King's Cross Central Limited Partnership)
Status: Completed in June 2012
Architect: Archer Humphryes Architects with Dexter Moran Associates
Structural and M&E engineer: Ramboll UK
Planning consultant: Argent (acting on behalf of King's Cross Central Limited Partnership)
Cost consultant: MDA
Contractor: Mace
Enabling and colonnade works: Allies & Morrison, Arup, Kier Wallis, KXC GP

THE BEAUMONT HOTEL 8 BALDERTON STREET, W1K

The project is a redevelopment of a Grade II listed, Art Deco former car park into a small, bespoke hotel, operated by Corbin & King Hotels. The scheme comprises 73 rooms, a spa, restaurant, bar, private residents lounge and conference room, and an inhabitable sculpture by Antony Gormley.

Estate: The Grosvenor Estate
Status: Under construction, due to complete Summer 2014
Architect: Reardon Smith Architects
Structural engineer: Ramboll UK
M&E engineer: Ramboll UK
Planning consultant: Gerald Eve
Project manager: Grosvenor
Cost consultant: EC Harris
Contractor: Chorus Group
Interior designer: Richmond International

THE CROWN & GREYHOUND PUB 73 DULWICH VILLAGE, SE21

The conversion and extension of the Crown & Greyhound Pub (Grade II Listed) to a boutique style 20-bedroom hotel located in the Dulwich Village Conservation Area. The former shuttle alley and coach house have been converted into bedrooms with a new garden bedroom wing to the rear.

Estate: The Dulwich Estate
Status: Planning granted March 2013, due to complete Spring 2015
Architect: EPR Architects
Structural engineer: Price & Myers
Planning consultant: Turley Associates
Agent for the Estate: Daniel Watney Chartered Surveyors
Transport: Mayer Brown Ltd

THE FIRE STATION 1 CHILTERN STREET, W1M

This Grade II listed former fire station built in 1889, will be converted into a 26-room luxury boutique hotel with the erection of a part three and five storey extension linking the main building with the ladder shed. The development includes a restaurant within the existing engine shed and a separate function room. The 1860s drill tower has been demolished and replaced with a three-storey extension whilst the perimeter walls, railings and doors have all been restored.

Estate: The Portman Estate
Status: Under construction, due to complete December 2013
Architect: David Archer Architects Ltd
Structural and M&E engineer: Ramboll UK Ltd
Planning consultant: Gerald Eve
Project manager and cost consultant: Baqus Group PLC
Contractor: Knight Harwood Ltd

QUEENSBRIDGE HOUSE 58-62 UPPER THAMES STREET, EC4

This 224-bed hotel, sited on the riverfront, will include a cocktail bar, reception rooms and apartments, along with a riverside restaurant and walkway. The building will replace three office buildings on a site that runs from Little Trinity Lane to the river, spanning Upper Thames Street.

Estate: The City of London Corporation
Status: Planning granted in March 2012
Architects: Bennetts Associates Architects and Dexter Moran Associates
Structural engineer: AKT II
M&E engineer: BSE3d
Planning consultant: Gerald Eve
Project manager: Jones Lang LaSalle
Cost consultant: Bradbrook Consultant

MASTERPLAN

CHOBHAM MANOR QUEEN ELIZABETH OLYMPIC PARK, STRATFORD, E20

Chobham Manor is the first of five neighbourhoods to be developed on Queen Elizabeth Olympic Park in Stratford, east London. Nestled between the East Village and Lee Valley VeloPark, it will comprise more than 800 homes, plus shops, community facilities and open spaces. There are five principal types of housing planned for Chobham Manor – townhouses, mews-style properties, maisonettes, mansions and apartments. Around 75 per cent of the homes will have three bedrooms or more to appeal to families, some properties will be designed for multiple generations of the same family, while 28 percent of homes will be affordable and shared ownership properties.

Estate: London Legacy Development Corporation
Status: Masterplan planning pending, Phase 1 first occupation in 2015
Architects: PRP, Make, Haworth Tompkins & Karakusevic-Carson
Structural engineer: Stephen Wilson Partnership
M&E engineer: Kaizenge
Planning consultant: Quod
Project manager & cost consultant: Taylor Wimpey
Developer: Taylor Wimpey & L&Q (Chobham Manor LLP)

EARLS COURT VISION SW5 / SW10

The proposals for Earls Court are based on the belief that urban developments should blend in with existing urban settings and become thriving, vibrant neighbourhoods. Inspired by the best characteristics of London, the Masterplan will transform the Earls Court & West Kensington Opportunity Area into a new urban district, creating four urban villages and a 21st century High Street. The design will provide sustainable urban living comprising 7,500 new homes, offices, hotels, work space, education and community facilities. A Cultural Strategy has been prepared as part of the planning applications, which will ensure that Earls Court's status as an important cultural and events destination will be preserved and enhanced.

Estate: Earls Court (Capital & Counties)
Status: Planning granted 2012, due to complete in 2030
Architects: Farrells, McAslan, Allies and Morrison, Studio Egret West, Benoy, Chris Dyson, KPF
Structural engineer: Arup
M&E consultant: Hoare Lea
Planning consultant: DP9
Project manager and cost consultant: EC Harris
Contractor: Sir Robert McAlpine
Landscape architects: Patel Taylor

KING'S CROSS CENTRAL MASTERPLAN N1

King's Cross Central is one of Europe's largest urban regeneration projects. The 24-hectare site is bordered by the new Eurostar line from France and bisected by Regent's Canal. The masterplan sets out a framework for the incremental development of a diverse mix of uses, embedded in one of the UK's most significant industrial heritage sites. These include 5.4 million square feet of office space, 2.2 million square feet of residential space and 1.1 million square feet of retail. A network of public open spaces-streets, lanes, squares and parks-permeate the urban blocks and make connections beyond the site.

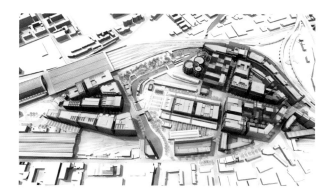

Estate: King's Cross (King's Cross Central Limited Partnership)
Date of completion: Masterplan completed 2007 ,
under construction
Masterplaners: Allies and Morrison with Porphyrios Associates
Structural & services engineer: Arup
Landscape architect: Townshend Landscape Architects

PEABODY 21ST CENTURY VISION WILD STREET, WC2B

Farrells worked with Peabody to develop a set of principles which illustrated how Peabody's 21st Century Vision could be delivered through spatial and physical design. Four existing estates were chosen as case studies for this research and were selected due to their varied architecture and the wide demographic they reflected: Wild Street Estate, Westminster; West Silverton, Newham; Pembury, Hackney and Rosendale & Peabody Hill, Lambeth. Particular areas of research included size of estate, location, ethnic diversity, unemployment levels, sustainable practices and existing community facilities. Farrells proposed that positive change could come about through space optimisation, alterations to the internal and external environment, resident engagement and building relationships with the local community. The proposals form the basis of how Peabody can deliver their mission in the 21st century, in both existing and new estates.

Estate: Peabody
Status: Feasibility study
Architect: Farrells

QUEEN ELIZABETH OLYMPIC PARK (LEGACY COMMUNITIES SCHEME)
STRATFORD, E20

The construction of five new neighbourhoods, each with its own distinct character, will see up to 8,000 homes being built in the Park by 2025. Planned around pocket parks and squares, and built to the latest standards of environmental sustainability, these neighbourhoods are being designed to rekindle the heritage of east London life, with its famous community spirit and vibrant cultural diversity, in homes that embrace and promote the most modern of living standards. The first of these neighbourhoods, Chobham Manor, will start to be built in early 2014.

Estate: London Legacy Development Corporation
Status: Outline Planning Permission granted Oct 2012, starting on site Jan 2014, due to complete December 2025

REGENT'S PLACE MASTERPLAN, RESIDENTIAL AND OFFICE BUILDINGS
NW1

The Regent's Place masterplan and commercial mixed use development successfully enhances and transforms the urban fabric of a key area of the West End of London bordering the Euston Road and Regent's Park. The brief was to create a diverse community and an integrated part of the West End of London. This was achieved by creating high quality spaces and places between the buildings, and a network of new streets, enabling and encouraging linkages to the surrounding area. The masterplan aims to re-establish the neighbourhood links through developing a commercial estate in an urban context for British Land with five new buildings completed in two phases.

Estate: Regent's Place (British Land)
Status: Masterplan completed 2010; Final phase of development (10 & 30 Brock Street and The Triton Building) due to complete 2013
Architects: Farrells, Wilkinson Eyre Architects, Carmody Groarke, Sheppard Robson, Stephen Marshall Architects (all designed buildings within the masterplan)
Structural engineer: Arup
Planning consultant: DP9

MIXED-USE

ARTHOUSE 1 YORK WAY, N1C

Designed by award-winning architects dRMM, this seven storey building comprises 143 intelligently planned apartments, 29 of which are affordable, in addition to commercial use at ground floor. At ground floor, a spacious lobby, landscaped courtyards and glazed cloisters connect the building with Handyside Park, a new green space designed by internationally acclaimed landscape architects Dan Pearson Studio. With views across Regent's Canal, Handyside Park and the listed Victorian East Handyside Canopy, ArtHouse offers ever-changing views of the city. Apartment interiors designed by Johnson Naylor, create bright and spacious living spaces, with a palette of quality materials and innovative, integrated storage.

Estate: King's Cross (King's Cross Central Limited Partnership)
Status: Under construction, due to complete October 2013
Architect: dRMM
Executive Architect: Weedon
Structural engineer: Arup
M&E engineer: Hoare Lea
Planning consultant: Argent
Project manager: King's Cross Central Limited Partnership
Cost consultant: Davis Langdon (an AECOM company)
Contractor: Kier
Interior architects: Johnson Naylor

11 BAKER STREET 11 BAKER STREET (PREVIOUSLY 7 – 17 BAKER STREET, 51 – 56 GEORGE STREET AND 26 – 31 PORTMAN CLOSE), W1U

Designed by Squire and Partners, this mixed-use site by Ahli United Bank has been redeveloped to comprise commercial offices over retail with residential accommodation along George Street.

Estate: The Portman Estate
Status: Completed in June 2011
Architect: Squire and Partners
Structural engineer: Cameron Taylor One
M&E engineer: Sinclair Knight Merz
Planning consultant: Gerald Eve
Project manager: GVA Second London Wall
Cost consultant: Rider Levett Bucknall
Contractor: McClarens

17-23 BENTINCK STREET MARYLEBONE, W1U

This scheme addresses an historic terrace of seven properties, with expiring leases coinciding. Retained facade proposals were originally seen as unacceptable in planning terms, but understanding their reasoning, the 'book-ends' of the development took on a refurbishment approach with No.17 becoming residential, and 'front rooms' reinstated at ground and first floor levels to avoid visible office lighting grids. The new build designs to the rear respect original plot widths, pulling and sinking planes to produce a rich articulation allowing oblique vistas throughout the levels, creating diverse character to the working environment despite the expansive floor plates. BREEAM excellent has been achieved, thanks to extensive areas of photovoltaic roof slates and 20 GSHP boreholes.

Estate: The Howard de Walden Estate
Status: Completed in August 2013
Architect: ESA architecture/design
Service engineer: RHB Partnership
Structural engineer: Elliott Wood
Main contractor: Volker Fitzpatrick
Project management: ESPM

BROMPTON QUARTER AND SOUTH KENSINGTON ESTATES SW7

Child Graddon Lewis have been appointed to assist in regenerating and re-positioning the image of the South Kensington Estate. Working closely with the estate, CGL have been designing improvements to the quality of the commercial units, many of which had not been fit for purpose for 21st century shops, cafes and restaurants. The estate has contributed to and benefited from the regeneration instigated by the public realm improvements to Exhibition Road and around South Kensington Station and continues to look for opportunities to create better buildings and spaces adjacent to one of the world's most significant cultural quarters.

Estate: South Kensington Estates
Status: Ongoing
Architect: Child Graddon Lewis
Structural engineers: Michael Barkley/ Abraham Consulting
Planning consultant: Gerald Eve
Project manager: HB Surveyors and Valuers

40 CHANCERY LANE 40-45 CHANCERY LANE, WC2A

This new building for developer Derwent London creates new office and retail space on a prominent corner site within the Chancery Lane Conservation Area. The scheme is carefully designed to respect adjacent listed buildings and acknowledge surrounding scale and materiality. A series of 1950/60s buildings on Chancery Lane and Cursitor Street are replaced with linked blocks separated by service cores rather than a single monolithic building. The 19th century building at 20-21 Took's Court is retained, with its facades restored. The historic street pattern of narrow passages leading to open spaces is reinforced with a public landscaped courtyard off Chancery Lane.

Estate: The Colville Estate
Status: Under construction , due to complete September 2014
Architect: Bennetts Associates Architects
Structural engineer: AKT II
Services engineer: Arup
Project manager: Buro Four
Cost consultant / QS: Davis Langdon
Contractor: Morgan Sindall
Landscape design: J+L Gibbons

100 CHEAPSIDE EC2V

100 Cheapside comprises the comprehensive redevelopment of a prominent site at the corner of King Street and Cheapside on the ceremonial route to and from the Guildhall. Offering Grade A office space and ground floor retail, the scheme is arranged on two basements, ground and nine upper floors and comprises a gross external area of circa 138,754 sq ft providing circa 12,939 sq ft net retail space and 86,159 sq ft net office accommodation, topped by a large roof terrace.

Estate: The City of London Corporation
Status: Planning granted, due to complete Autumn 2014
Architect: EPR Architects
Structural engineer: Waterman Structures
M&E engineer: Hilson Moran
Planning consultant: DP9
Project manager: GVA Second London Wall
Cost consultant: Quantem
Contractor: Skanska
CDM-C: RFL

33 DAVIES STREET W1K

This new six storey building, offering prime office space and retail units, is located on Mayfair's principal thoroughfares of Davies Street and Grosvenor Street. The building uses a traditional hand- made brick and Portland stone in its stately 45-metre facade and prime retail frontage, its height sympathetically reflecting the historical streetscape. In addition to 2,680 square metres of office space there are two retail units comprising 708 sqm on the ground floor and basement, with an additional space available on the first floor. Each unit is provided with a dedicated, independently metered utility electrical service and independent alarm systems from the rest of the building.

Estate: The Grosvenor Estate
Clients: The Grosvenor Estate & Stow
Status: Under construction, due to complete January 2014
Architect: HOK
Structural engineer: Ramboll
M&E engineer: MTT
Planning consultant: Gerald Eve
Project manager: Grosvenor
Cost consultant: Davis Langdon
Contractor: Sir Robert McAlpine

12-18 DEVONSHIRE STREET W1

A discerning Grade II listed Portland Stone faced terrace to the west of Portland Place saw its original turn of the century leases expiring in the same period. No.12, a former Embassy, was refurbished and extended with a new third floor, for office use, whilst the rest of the terrace was extensively refurbished with contemporary in-fill extensions at ground and basement levels, all destined for medical use. Sensitive contemporary design now sits beside original lift cars and grand staircases; ingenious discrete servicing routes provide a new lease of life for the next century.

Estate: The Howard de Walden Estate
Status: Completed in March 2013
Architect: ESA architecture/design
Services engineer: RHB Partnership LLP
Structural engineer: Richard Watkins & Associates
Project manager: ESPM

GILLENDER STREET BROMLEY-BY-BOW, E3

Sun Flour Mill in Bromley-by-Bow is a new mixed-use, residential-led development of 109 units within the Limehouse Cut Conservation Area, recently granted planning permission. Comprising three buildings of one, two and three-bedroom units, with commercial space at ground floor replacing the existing employment use on the site, the scheme sits adjacent to the River Lea and the Lime House Cut canal at the Bow locks. The residential element, which includes 35 per cent affordable housing, will be managed by the Peabody Trust. The Allies and Morrison building forms respond to the complex geometry of the site, reflected in the plan and roof form.

Estate: Peabody
Status: Planning granted
Architect: Allies and Morrison
Structural engineer: Adams Kara Taylor
Service engineer: Good Design Practice

GRIDIRON ONE PANCRAS SQUARE, N1C

This Grade A office building has a prime spot at the gateway to the King's Cross development: the underground entrance is in the building itself. The building, designed by award winning David Chipperfield Architects, has iron twisted columns to reflect the Victorian heritage of the site. Gridiron is approximately 55,120 square feet over eight floors. A typical floor is 7,050 square feet with 600 square feet of south facing balconies. A through-reception can be accessed either from the main entrance on Pancras Square or from King's Boulevard, with shops and cafes housed at street level. Goods and services for this building are delivered below street level via a shared access route.

Estate: King's Cross (King's Cross Central Limited Partnership)
Status: Under construction, due to complete December 2013
Architect: David Chipperfield Architects
Structural engineer: AKT
M&E engineer: Grontmij
Planning consultant: Argent
Project manager: King's Cross Central Limited Partnership
Cost consultant: Gardiner and Theobold
Contractor: Bam

62 GREEN STREET 62 GREEN STREET & 30 NORTH AUDLEY STREET, W1K

The development includes the conversion of a high street bank to a residential and retail scheme, comprising nine apartments on the upper floors and a restaurant at ground and basement. The apartments include three triplex penthouses ranging in size from 1,650 square feet to 2,500 square feet each with a private roof terrace. Key features include floor to ceiling windows offering volume and light as prominent characteristics of the development and an interesting use of space to compliment the original architecture.

Estate: The Grosvenor Estate
Status: Completed in February 2012
Architect: Latitude Architects
Structural engineer: Hurst Pierce & Malcolm
M&E engineer: Mecserve
Planning consultant: Gerald Eve
Project manager: Grosvenor
Cost consultant: Thompson Cole
Contractor: Chorus

18-20 GROSVENOR STREET W1

This new 40,699 square foot building incorporates a retained Bath stone facade alongside contemporary interior design over five floors, including open plan Grade A offices and two retail occupiers, aiming to achieve BREEAM Excellent rating and an EPC rating of B. Designed by BFLS Architects, it will be a flagship project adding to the area with a distinct identity and character. The architectural and design specification incorporates flexible, large floor plates, including a separate room with period features on each floor, good floor to ceiling heights, and also a large reception and outdoor rooftop entertaining space, with discreet access on Brooks Mews.

Estate: The Grosvenor Estate
Status: Under Construction, due to complete January 2015
Architect: Flanegan Lawrence (previously BFLS)
Structural and M&E engineer: Ramboll UK
Planning consultant: Gerald Eve
Project manager: Grosvenor
Cost consultant: EC Harris
Contractor: Sir Robert McAlpine

KING'S CROSS BUILDING B4 KING'S CROSS CENTRAL, N1 C

Building B4 is one of three new office buildings that form a part of the masterplan for King's Cross Central. The buildings look onto two new public spaces – Pancras Square and the King's Boulevard. It provides 130,000 sq ft net Grade A office space above retail and restaurant uses. The facades are composed from a white precast stone outer masonry layer, behind which sits a fine metal and glass inner layer. As the building rises, the masonry window surrounds become more delicate, whilst the inner glass layer recedes into the building. At the final floor it is completely absent, revealing a glimpse of sky. Sustainability has been central to the development of the King's Cross masterplan and, as such, Building B4 is enabled for a BREEAM 2011 rating of Outstanding.

Estate: King's Cross (King's Cross Central Limited Partnership)
Status: Under construction
Architect: Allies and Morrison
Structural engineer: AKTII
Services engineer: Grontmij
Quantity surveyor: Davis Langdon
Landscape: Townshend Landscape Architects
Contractor: BAM

LISCARTAN & GRANVILLE HOUSES 127/135 SLOANE STREET, SW1X

The development at 127-135 Sloane Street is a 12,500 square metre mixed-use office and retail scheme, including a six-storey sandstone faced retail and office building on Sloane Street, along with smaller retail units and a restaurant onto Pavilion Road faced with hand-made brick. Landscaped terraces and a courtyard accommodate the change in scale from the office building to the scale of the mews. A shallow broad stair from Pavilion Road invites public access to the landscaped courtyard that is surrounded with retail units and a restaurant. The design has achieved a BREEAM Excellent rating.

Estate: The Cadogan Estate
Status: Under construction, due to complete January 2015
Architect: Stiff+Trevillion
Structural engineer: AKTII
Building services: Hoare Lea
Quantity surveyor: The Trevor Patrick Partnership
Project manager: Capital and Provincial
Main contractor: Mace Ltd

MARBLE ARCH HOUSE 32 – 50 EDGWARE ROAD, 66 – 68 SEYMOUR STREET, 5 SEYMOUR PLACE AND 12 – 13 HAMPDEN GURNEY STREET, W2

Occupying a prominent corner position on Seymour Street on the western edge of Marylebone in London's West End, this scheme proposes a new modern office building with its entrance on Seymour Street and new retail accommodation at ground floor fronting Edgware Road. Situated at the western 'gateway' of the Estate, it is hoped to set a quality benchmark for its ongoing and long-term strategic development. The comprehensive proposals include the reconfiguration and extension of 62 – 64 Seymour Street to provide a new restaurant at ground floor with high quality private residential apartments on the upper floors. The mixed use scheme proposes circa 91,000 sq ft of net internal floor space divided between offices, retail, restaurant and residential.

Estate: The Portman Estate
Status: Under construction, due to complete November 2013
Developer: British Land
Architect: Bennetts Associates Architects

MITRE SQUARE EC3

This new 273,000 square foot building will provide Category A office space built over the two lower ground floors, ground and sixteen upper floors, along with ground floor retail. The building form responds to the tight planning constraints of the area and the adjacent urban fabric, which contains a mix of uses including a school, offices, and residential buildings. Demolition commenced in June 2013.

Estate: The City of London Corporation
Status: Planning granted June 2011
Architect: Sheppard Robson
Developer: Helical Bar
Structural engineer: Ramboll
M&E engineer: Robert Preston & Partners
Planning consultant: DP9
Project manager: GVA Second London Wall
Contractor: Keltbray Ltd (Demo)

ONE EAGLE PLACE SW1Y 6AF

Standing in a prime location, with facades on Piccadilly and Jermyn Street, Eagle Place is a development providing premium West End office accommodation alongside premium residential and flagship retail space. This key development from The Crown Estate, in partnership with the Healthcare of Ontario Pension Plan (HOOPP) and Stanhope, elegantly incorporates original retained facades with contemporary design by the highly acclaimed Eric Parry Architects. It is the first of a series of major developments in St James's as part of The Crown Estate's £500m investment vision for the area.

Estate: The Crown Estate
Status: Completed in July 2013
Architect: Eric Parry Architects
Structural engineer: Waterman Structures
M&E engineer: Mecserve
Planning consultant: CBRE
Cost consultant: Gardiner & Theobald
Contractor: Stanhope
Construction managers: Lend Lease

ONE VINE STREET REGENT STREET, W1J

One Vine Street is the first completed building within the Quadrant masterplan, a two-hectare site which straddles the south-eastern end of Regent Street adjacent to Piccadilly Circus. Four levels of commercial offices are set above a single large retail space which is capable of subdivision at basement, ground and first floors. Duplex residential apartments occupy the roof space of the stone-dressed crescent. New facades are in hand-made bricks and Portland stone, with natural slate and lead roofs. The entrance to the building is through the retained facade of a former public house and leads to a small atrium lined with vertical timber battens and linear lighting.

Estate: The Crown Estate
Status: Completed in 2008
Architect: Allies and Morrison
Structural engineer: Waterman Partnership
Services engineer: Mecserve
Quantity surveyor: Gardiner and Theobald
Contractor: Sir Robert McAlpine

PORTMAN MEWS SOUTH REDEVELOPMENT 3-7 PORTMAN MEWS SOUTH, W1H

A mixed-use commercial office and retail / restaurant development of around 2,200 square metres located between Oxford Street and Portman Square, has involved the demolition of a group of period buildings within the Portman Conservation Area and replacement with a new commercial building arranged over five levels. The office element on the upper floors is served by a single core, with a large restaurant at ground floor and basement level. The elevations are designed to retain the vertical character of the former collection of buildings and enhance the historic architectural setting.

Estate: The Portman Estate
Status: Completed in October 2011
Architect: Garnett+Partners LLP
Structural engineer: URS Global Operations
M&E engineer: Max Fordham LLP

10 PORTMAN SQUARE (PREVIOUSLY 2 – 14 BAKER STREET), W1M

This mixed-use building will provide 133,425 sq ft of high quality office and retail space on a prominent site on the corner of Portman Square. The typical level provides a column-free floor plate of over 18,330 sqft which is unusual in the context of the West End. The perceived scale of the building is broken down into smaller constituent elements, fitting of the local area, each of them individually enriched with high quality materials such as stone, bronzed metal and dichroic glass. The building is designed to achieve a BREEAM Excellent, and uses ground-sourced heat pumps and solar panels to reduce its carbon footprint.

Estate: The Portman Estate
Status: Completed 2013
Architect: Jestico + Whiles
Developer: British Land PLC

QUADRANT 3 AIR STREET, W1

Located on the site of the former Regent Palace hotel, Quadrant 3 is a vibrant building featuring a rich mixture of retained neo-classical facades and contemporary architecture. In a prime location overlooking Piccadilly Circus, Quadrant 3 forms part of a comprehensive restoration and redevelopment of the four quadrant blocks at the southern end of Regent Street. The Quadrant scheme puts sustainability at the heart of its design and provides significantly improved public realm. To date, it has won over 10 awards, including Best Historic Building Management at the London Planning Awards 2013.

Estate: The Crown Estate
Status: Completed in November 2011
Architect: Dixon Jones Architects
Structural engineer: Waterman
M&E engineer: Aecom
Planning consultant: CBRE
Cost consultant: Davis Langdon
Development manager: Stanhope
Construction manager: Sir Robert McAlpine
Public realm: Atkins
Historic architect: Donald Insall Associates
Residential designer: Johnson Naylor

REGENT STREET W4 & W5 SOUTH REGENT STREET, W1

Together, blocks W4 and W5 south renew two prestigious central London sites to create world-class, state-of-the art retail and office accommodation. The curved 'tulip' profiles of the two new structures sit behind four Grade II listed and retained facades on Regent and New Burlington streets, tapering towards the sky to form distinctive new contributions to the neighbourhood's built heritage. Setbacks at ground level create two crisply defined bases that address and improve the public realm. Combined, the inserted elements will offer more than 200,000 sq ft of Class A office space above 100,000 sq ft of retail, full-height atriums and a connected string of external courtyards.

Estate: The Crown Estate
Status: Under construction, due to complete in 2015
Development manager: Exemplar Properties Development
Architect: Allford Hall Monaghan Morris
Structural engineer: Waterman Group
M&E engineer: Watkins Payne Partnership

THE CHELSEA CINEMA 196 – 222 KINGS ROAD, SW3

The Cadogan Estate are looking to reinvigorate and improve this Kings Road site through the creation of a landmark development incorporating retail, office, cinema, public house, roof top restaurant, affordable and market residential with landscaped courtyard. Inspired by the site's existing 1930s buildings, the design has evolved to encompass art deco nuances through contemporary interpretation. An asymmetric mansard roof-scape ties this landmark building into the surrounding environment, while significant enhancement to the rear of the site improves the public realm. An accented contextual material palette seeks to provide a distinct and characterful streetscape, reinforcing the Kings Road as a high quality shopping destination.

Estate: The Cadogan Estate
Status: Stage C, due to complete in 2017
Architect: Paul Davis + Partners
Structural engineer: AKT II
M&E engineer: Hurley Palmer Flatt
Planning consultant: Gerald Eve
Project manager: Capital and Provincial
Cost consultant: The Trevor Patrick Partnership

SEVEN PANCRAS SQUARE AND STANLEY BUILDING N1C

This Grade A office building has an unrivalled location at the gateway to King's Cross, framing the new Battlebridge Place. Designed by Studio Downie Architects, Seven Pancras Square consists of a new build office wrapping around the existing Grade II Listed Stanley Building, with approximately 19,700 sq ft net of office and retail space over five floors. The building will contain a striking lightwell between the new and old spaces and will also bring the original Victorian roof terrace back into use atop of the Stanley Building. The building will be home to contemporary serviced office provider, The Office Group.

Estate: King's Cross (King's Cross Central Limited Partnership)
Status: Under construction, due to complete Q3 2014
Architect: Studio Downie Architects
Structural engineer: Arup
M&E engineer: Scotch Partners
Planning consultant: Argent
Project manager: King's Cross Central Limited Partnership
Cost consultant: Davis Langdon (an AECOM company)
Contractor: BAM

SMITHFIELD GENERAL MARKET & ANNEXE EC1

This scheme comprises 21 shops, a public piazza and offices behind retained buildings, integrating large-scale office floor plates into the historic grain, while preserving the existing buildings. The General Market perimeter buildings and existing facades of the Red House, former Fish Market and Engine House, will be restored and accompanied by the new developments, bringing the structures into viable current use. The design aims to achieve BREEAM 'Excellent', and should be available to tenants from Spring 2017.

Estate: The City of London Corporation
Status: Planning under review
Developer: Henderson Global Investors
Architect: John McAlsan & Partners
Structural Engineer: AKT II
M&E Engineer: Long and Partners
Planning Consultant: DPQ
Cost Consultant: EC Harris

ST JAMES'S MARKET REGENT STREET/HAYMARKET, SW1

St James's Market is one of The Crown Estate's most ambitious redevelopment schemes to date. The scheme takes its name from the now lost area of St James's Market, which between the 17th and 19th centuries offered a spacious street of inns, entertainment, and a busy hay and straw market. Located between Haymarket and Regent Street, it will provide world-class architecture with preserved historic facades, bringing the area back into line with the quality of historic St James's. The scheme will also see transformational public realm developments to create a new pedestrian quarter in London's West End.

Estate: The Crown Estate
Status: Planning granted January 2013, due to complete late 2015
Architect: Make Architects

WALKER'S COURT W1F

This comprehensive redevelopment of Walker's Court will replace entrenched illegal sex shops with a restaurant, a 155 seat cabaret theatre, retail and nightclub uses, and Soho Estates's headquarter offices. The proposed scheme will enhance the architectural features of Walker's Court, reduce the opportunity for criminal activity and brighten the atmosphere of a sometimes intimidating alley. The Raymond Revuebar neon sign will be painstakingly repaired and reinstated. The handsome buildings within the development will be restored while buildings past their useful economic life will be replaced with exceptional architecture. Those buildings that must remain will have fins mounted on the elevations echoing the shape of the buildings behind.

Estate: Soho Estates
Status: Design stage. Planning to be submitted September 2013, due to complete July 2015
Architect: Matt Architecture / soda
Structural engineer: Tier Consult London
M&E engineer: Thornton Reynolds
Planning consultant: Gerald Eve
Project manager: Development Managers Limited
Cost consultant: Gleeds

WARDOUR STREET 54-58 WARDOUR STREET AND 74-76 OLD COMPTON STREET, W1D

This scheme will refurbish and remodel the upper floors to produce contemporary office space with a part given over to residential use, and add a two-storey extension to the Bourchier Street frontage to create duplex residential flats. The Bourchier Street corner will be in-filled with a two-storey brass facade inset with a portrait window with views along Brewer Street. The Bourchier Street extension will be faced with brass fins to echo the corner in-fill. The development will be carried out with the three ground floor tenants (restaurant, café and shop) remaining in situ and operating. The completed development will provide eight one-bed flats together with the office space.

Estate: Soho Estates
Status: Design stage. Planning to be submitted September 2013, due to complete April 2015
Architect: Berman Guedes Stretton
Structural engineer: Tier Consult London
M&E engineer: Thornton Reynolds
Planning consultant: Gerald Eve
Project manager: Development Managers Limited
Cost consultant: Academy Consulting Solutions

70 WIGMORE STREET W1U

Now affectionately known as 'The Triangle,' seven historic addresses have been combined in this office development with retail and cafe uses at ground and basement levels. The historic Wigmore Street facades, together with part of that to Marylebone Lane have been retained; the northern-most corner and facades to Jason Court are then contemporary new-build, the latter incorporating a text based public art over which particular care has been exercised. Utilising Air Source Heat Pumps, the project delivers a BREEAM rating of Very Good.

Estate: The Howard de Walden Estate
Status: Completed in October 2011
Architect: ESA architecture/design
Services engineer: Scott Wilson
Structural engineer: Buro Happold
Project manager/QS: Jones Lang LaSalle
Main contractor: Mansell Plc

PUBLIC REALM

BROADGATE CIRCLE, CITY OF LONDON EC2M

Works are currently underway to refurbish and transform Broadgate Circle into a new civic space at the heart of Broadgate. The scheme designed by Arup Associates will be simple and elegant in design, and sensitive to the original character of the Circle, whilst improving circulation, visual coherence and emphasising the unique civic qualities of the Circle. A stronger and more diverse retail offer is proposed, including seven new units at lower ground level arranged radially around a performance space. Four new kiosks will be created at ground level, two of which form entrances to the reconfigured first floor bar restaurant and terraces.

Estate: Broadgate (British Land and Blackstone)
Status: Under construction, due to complete Easter 2015
Architect: Arup Associates
Structural and M&E engineer: Arup Associates
Planning consultant: DP9
Project manager: M3 Consulting
Cost consultant: Mace Cost Consulting
Contractor: Mace

BROWN HART GARDENS MAYFAIR, W1K

Brown Hart Gardens is a Grade II listed electricity substation, dating from 1903, beneath a raised hard landscaped deck which is a privately owned space with public access. The project aims to breathe new life into a much-loved historic neighbourhood building. The interventions celebrate and dramatise improved access. Flexible planting and seating together with a new cafe, designed to be transparent and evoke the forms of the original building, provide facilities for relaxation, recreation and community events.

Estate: The Grosvenor Estate
Status: Completed in July 2013
Architect: BDP
Structural engineer: Hurst Pierce and Malcolm LLP
M&E engineer: Edward Pearce LLP
Planning consultant: Gerald Eve LLP
Project manager: Grosvenor
Cost consultant: Gardiner & Theobald LLP
Contractor: Chorus

CARNABY ECHOES W1F

Renowned British artist Lucy Harrison has been commissioned by Shaftesbury PLC to create a new installation to reflect the rich cultural heritage of the area surrounding Carnaby Street in London. Curated by Futurecity, her ambitious project consists of a walking tour and exhibition of photography, film, audio and archive materials which viewers are guided through by an app and commemorative plaques, from 1930s jazz clubs such as the Nest and the Florence Mills Social Parlour, to the introduction of Ska to the UK by Count Suckle and Duke Vin at the Roaring Twenties Club in the 1960s. Weaving together a century of memories and narratives that Harrison has spent over a year unearthing, her project includes contributions from Boy George, Pete Townshend, Mark Ellen, Lloyd Coxsone and Dynamo.

Estate: Shaftesbury PLC
Status: Opening September 2013
Artist: Lucy Harrison
Curator: Futurecity
carnabyechoes.com
#CarnabyEchoes

CULTURAL PLACEMAKING STRATEGY FOR EARLS COURT SW5 / SW10

Developed in 2010 by Futurecity, this Cultural Placemaking Strategy outlines an approach for embedded public art and cultural programming across the Earls Court Scheme. It proposes ideas, themes and milestones for key areas for the successful delivery and ownership of a series of high profile cultural and creative programmes, each subtly defining the key character of each village. This strategy is underpinned by the belief that culture, creativity and public art have to demonstrate an understanding of the ambition of Earls Court and the communities that choose to locate there, therefore this strategy also outlines ways in which EC&O Properties will work closely with leading cultural organisations and stakeholders from the outset.

Estate: Earls Court (Capital & Counties Properties PLC, 'Capco')
Status: Planning consent granted November 2012, approved by the mayor in July 2013
Author: Futurecity
Consultant: Future Creative
Education and engagements: Future Creative
Contributor: Andrew McIlroy

ELIZABETH STREET BELGRAVIA, SW1W

The proposal sought to reduce traffic domination, de-clutter the public realm, enhance the quality of public realm and strengthen the special urban village atmosphere of this distinctive local retail destination. Utilising a palette of high quality and robust materials, trees and street furniture have been introduced to form a seamless floorscape and street elevation that complements, rather than competes with, the scale and nature of Elizabeth Street and its buildings. It has also helped to ensure that they relate to, and enrich, the character of Elizabeth Street, and will simplify long-term management and maintenance. Elizabeth Street has won several awards and sets a precedent for future projects.

Estate: The Grosvenor Estate
Status: Completed in September 2010
Architect: BDP
Structural & M&E engineer: BDP / Skanska
Project manager & cost consultant: Gardiner & Theobald LLP
Transport consultant: MVA Consultancy
Contractor: Skanska

GASHOLDER NO. 8 REGENT'S CANAL, N1C

The iconic gasholders have been residents of King's Cross for over 150 years. Originally constructed in the 1850s, Gasholder No. 8 is a Grade II listed structure. Its 25 metre high circular frame has been painstakingly dismantled and has been refurbished in Yorkshire. 2013 sees it return to King's Cross, where it is currently being re-located on the north side of the Regent's Canal. The gasholder guide frame will sit in new landscaping with paths leading down to the canal towpath and a circular pavilion with a landscaped centre, designed by Bell Philips Architects will form a public park within the structure.

Estate: King's Cross (King's Cross Central Limited Partnership)
Status: Under construction, outline planning consent December 2006
Architect: Bell Phillips Architects
Structural engineer: Arup
Planning consultant: Argent
Project manager: King's Cross Central Limited Partnership
Cost consultant: Davis Langdon (an AECOM company)
Lighting designer: Speirs & Major
Landscape designers: Townshend Landscape Architects and Dan Pearson Studio

GRANARY SQUARE N1C

This is London's newest square and one of the largest of its kind in Europe, built where barges once unloaded their goods. This aquatic history has been worked into the new design, which is animated with over 1,000 choreographed fountains – each individually lit. The square is surrounded by historic buildings - giving the space atmosphere and character. Wide, south-facing steps sweep down to Regent's Canal. Opened in June 2012, Granary Square has already played host to the musical festivals Traction and Africa Express, as well as The Big Dance and even an ice cream festival.

Estate: King's Cross (King's Cross Central Limited Partnership)
Status: Completed in June 2012
Architect: TLA
Structural & M&E engineer: PBA
Planning consultant: Argent
Project manager: King's Cross Central Limited Partnership
Cost consultant: Davis Langdon (an AECOM company)
Contractor: BAM Nuttall
Fountains: The Fountain Workshop
Paving: Miller Druck
Trees: Willerbys

LONDON 2012 MASTERPLAN STRATFORD, E20

Having helped assess the regeneration potential of the Lower Lea Valley and contributed to London's successful bid to host the 2012 Games, Allies and Morrison subsequently became a part of a multi-disciplinary team appointed by the Olympic Delivery Authority to deliver masterplans for the Olympic and Paralympic Games, and for the Post-Games Transformation of the site in 2013, creating a new park for London. The practice are also the design architects for new structures, bridges and highways in the park, leading the design overlay of the public areas of the Olympic Park for use during the Games as well as a number of other key historic London venues with the London Organising Committee of the Olympic Games (LOCOG), as part of Team Populous. In 2008 Allies and Morrison were appointed by the LDA to jointly lead the masterplan for permanent Legacy development and are now working on this with the Olympic Park Legacy Company.

Estate: London Legacy Development Corporation
Status: Completed in 2012
Architect: Allies and Morrison, as part of Team Populous
Landscape Design: Hargreaves Associates-LdA design
Structural and Civil Engineers: Buro Happold, Arup, Atkins

MAYFAIR AND BELGRAVIA PUBLIC REALM HANDBOOK MAYFAIR AND BELGRAVIA

A key challenge that the Mayfair and Belgravia Estates face today is their domination by traffic and its associated clutter of signage and infrastructure. To resolve this, BDP worked with Grosvenor in liaison with WCC, to develop a Public Realm Handbook containing principles and design guidance for improving the public realm and continuous enhancement of both estates. This handbook translates broader strategic advice into a delivery mechanism for the innovative design and implementation of schemes and will, over time, lead to wholesale coordinated improvements to streets and spaces in Mayfair and Belgravia and once again make them better places for people.

Estate: The Grosvenor Estate
Status: Ongoing
Architect: BDP
Transport consultant: MVA Consultancy

MOUNT STREET MAYFAIR, W1K

Undertaken in partnership with Westminster City Council, these proposals sought to revive the grandeur of this beautiful street by improving the pedestrian experience and reducing traffic domination. This was achieved by installing high quality and robust surfacing materials and by strengthening physical and visual links to adjacent green spaces. Through careful consideration of materials sympathetic to the historic context of Mayfair, contemporary design principles, collaboration with artist Tadao Ando (commissioned for his sculpture/ water feature 'Silence') and close liaison with local residents, retailers and landowners, Mount Street and Carlos Place have undergone a dramatic transformation to become an international destination and 'place for people' recognised in the receipt of the prestigious Civic Trust Award.

Estate: The Grosvenor Estate
Status: Completed in December 2010
Architect: BDP
Structural & M&E engineers: BDP / Skanska
Project manager & cost consultant: Gardiner & Theobald LLP
Transport consultant: MVA Consultancy
Contractor: Skanska

NORTH AUDLEY STREET (PHASES 1 & 3) MAYFAIR, W1K

These proposals sought to address traffic domination, and convert this busy thoroughfare into a place with greater priority for people, reviving the identity of this beautiful street. The design improved the pedestrian experience by installing high quality and robust surfacing materials and by strengthening physical and visual links to adjacent spaces whilst allowing for potential future two-way traffic. Through careful consideration of materials sympathetic to its historic context, contemporary design principles, incorporation of special public art coal holes and close liaison with key stakeholders, North Audley Street has undergone a dramatic transformation and defined its sense of place as a key street in Mayfair.

Estate: The Grosvenor Estate
Status: Completed in June 2012
Architect: BDP
Structural and M&E engineer: BDP / West One
Project manager and cost consultant: Gardiner & Theobald LLP
Transport consultant: Urban Flow
Contractor: West One

OXFORD CIRCUS W1

Through creating two new diagonal pedestrian crossings, pedestrian crossing times have been reduced by 52 seconds, with straight across crossings realigned to better serve the pedestrian desire lines with narrowed central islands. The removal of nearly half the street furniture along with 500 metres of footway widening on Regent Street, both north and south of the junction, has created 63 per cent more usable space for pedestrians, and has also improved bus lanes on the Regent Street approaches. The closure of Princes Street and Little Argyll Street, two side streets south of the Oxford Circus junction, has smoothed traffic flow through the junction.

Estate: The Crown Estate
Status: Completed in November 2010
Landscape Architect: Atkins
Structural & M&E engineer, project manager, cost consultant & contractor: West One
Planning Consultant: Atkins/ CBRE
Highways and Transport: Atkins

PORTMAN SQUARE W1M

This scheme seeks to make this busy square more pedestrian-friendly by rationalising the carriageway, widening the footway around the square and aligning the kerbs to attain a new symmetry, and also widening the footway along Seymour Street in front of the Churchill Hotel. Aiming to provide a safer and more accessible pedestrian environment, the scheme includes updated pedestrian crossing facilities at junctions around the square and four oasis areas at each corner, utilising good quality materials and public art. Existing lighting has been upgraded to comply with current standards, whilst cyclists are catered for by a provision of space for the Barclays Cycle Hire Scheme.

Estate: The Portman Estate
Status: Completed in June 2013
Planning consultant & contractor: British Land

QUADRANT GLASSHOUSE STREET, AIR STREET, SHERWOOD STREET, W1

The Quadrant public realm scheme aims to create an active ground-floor frontage accommodating new shops and other facilities, transforming previously underused and run-down streets around the building into a vibrant part of the West End. This has been brought about through the pedestrianisation of most of Glasshouse Street, the installation of a 12,000 square foot, off street service yard, and a new pedestrian arcade called 'Wilder Walk' linking the south-west end of Denman Street to Glasshouse Street, housing a new piece of public art.

Estate: The Crown Estate
Status: Completed in June 2013
Landscape architect: Atkins
Structural & M&E engineer, cost consultant & contractor: West One
Planning Consultant: Atkins
Project Manager: Westminster City Council Project Board/ West One
Highway and transport: Atkins

ST. JAMES'S GATEWAY PUBLIC REALM EAGLE PLACE AND JERMYN STREET, PICCADILLY, W1

Forming an integral part of the new St James's Gateway building by Eric Parry, this project encompassed the public realm improvement works to Eagle Place and part of Jermyn Street, involving the repaving of the perimeter streets with York stone, the sensitive restoration of gas lamps and the removal of phone boxes that had attracted anti-social behaviour to the area. New public artwork, including the 'sculptural comic' cornice by Richard Deacon and the bust of the late Sir Simon Milton former deputy mayor and leader of Westminster City Council on the corner of One Eagle Place, the site of his first London office, seek to reinforce community connections.

Estate: The Crown Estate
Status: Completed in June 2013
Landscape architect & highways and transport: Atkins
Structural engineer: Waterman
M&E engineer: Mecserve
Planning consultant: Atkins/ CBRE
Project manager & cost consultant: Gardiner and Theobald
Contractor: Lend Lease

STUDY FOR THE BAKER STREET QUARTER EUSTON ROAD, NW1

This study for the Baker Street Quarter examines the public realm on Marylebone Road, with specific attention to Baker Street tube station forecourt and concourse level, Baker Street North, Allsop Place South and the Madame Tussauds corner. Taking into consideration Baker Street Station's strategic position, the study looks at ways to regenerate the gateway to Marylebone for visitors, businesses, residents and students. The station is a principal civic space for the Baker Street Quarter, and improvements to the public realm and frontage would reconnect it with the city and surrounding communities, including the adjacent Regent's Park Crown Estate and the Howard De Walden Estate.

Estate: The Portman Estate
Status: Feasibility study
Architect: Farrells

TWO-WAY PICCADILLY – '2WP' PHASE 01 PICCADILLY, PICCADILLY CIRCUS, ST. JAMES'S STREET, PALL MALL, W1

The Piccadilly Two Way Phase 1 scheme aims to redress the balance between pedestrians and vehicles so that Piccadilly, Piccadilly Circus and St. James's Street fulfill their purpose as shopping areas of international recognition and improve the ambience. The scheme promotes Piccadilly, Piccadilly Circus and St. James's Street as successful shopping environments with greater freedom to move between shops and cultural uses, with a reduction in the noise, smell, danger and disruption caused by traffic, and also improves the attractiveness of arrival points across St. James's, Mayfair and the whole Piccadilly and Regent Street corridors to all their streets and spaces.

Estate: The Crown Estate
Clients: The Crown Estate, City of Westminster and Transport for London
Status: Completed in 2011
Landscape architect & planning consultant: Atkins
Structural & M&E engineer, cost consultant & contractor: West One
Project manager: Westminster City Council Project Board/ West One
Detailed traffic design: SKM Colin Buchanan

TWO-WAY PICCADILLY – '2WP' PHASE 02 REGENT STREET, ST. JAMES'S, WATERLOO PLACE, HAYMARKET, W1

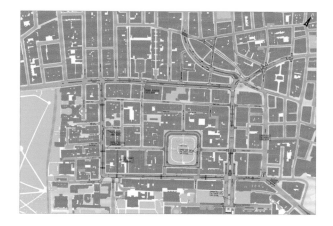

The Piccadilly Two Way Phase 2 scheme aims to enhance views and improve the setting of key buildings and the sense of place to 'civilise' the streets, whilst providing more space for pedestrians, improving legibility and accessibility for pedestrians along desire lines and increasing connectivity through a safer cycling environment, improved resilience of the district's highway network and bus reliability. It will continue to allow servicing, delivering and parking for local businesses, residents and visitors, and will maintain post Piccadilly Two Way traffic patterns, flow and provide network resilience

Estate: The Crown Estate
Clients: The Crown Estate, City of Westminster and TfL
Status: Completed in September 2013
Landscape architect & planning consultant: Atkins
Structural & M&E engineer, cost consultant & contractor: West One
Project Manager: Westminster City Council Project Board/ West One
Detailed traffic design: SKM Colin Buchanan

RESIDENTIAL

33 CADOGAN SQUARE 33 CADOGAN SQUARE AND 132 PAVILION ROAD, SW1X

Smallwood Architects Ltd have been appointed lead consultant by The Cadogan Estate to provide architectural services for the refurbishment and alteration of the house and mews to a very high standard, sufficient to satisfy the demands of a potential client purchaser at the top end of the residential market. The requirement is to provide designs and documentation to encompass a fully considered scheme sufficient for Planning and Listed Building Consent to be obtained.

Estate: The Cadogan Estate
Status: Design stage
Architect: Smallwood Architects Ltd
Structural engineer: Trigram Partnership Consulting Structural Engineers
M&E engineer: Qoda Consulting Ltd
Planning consultant: Gerald Eve
Historic buildings consultant: Donald Insall Associates

23-25 CASTLEREAGH STREET W1H

Paul Davis + Partners obtained planning permission to develop Castle House in the West End into a scheme of eight apartments and two courtyard houses that will replace a derelict building in a quiet street in Marylebone. The development, which will be Code 4 for Sustainable Homes, will be built with SIP panels and include green roofs and PV panels. The south facing common stair landings will be open to a green courtyard. This will be the third project Paul Davis + Partners have built for The Portman Estate.

Estate: The Portman Estate
Status: Under construction , due to complete August 2014
Architect: Paul Davis + Partners
Structural engineer: Furness Partnership
M&E engineer: Crofton Design
Planning consultant: Gerald Eve
Project manager & cost consultant: Potter Raper Partnership
Contractor: Kind and Company (Builders) Limited

DUKE STREET APARTMENTS 55-73 DUKE STREET, W1K

A Grade II listed development recently refurbished to create 16 brand new, high-end rental apartments across two buildings. Located in North Mayfair, Duke Street provides a mixture of local restaurants, cafes and amenities, recently complemented by Grosvenor's neighbouring public realm works including the restoration of Brown Hart Gardens. The thoughtfully designed apartments carefully combine historic features and contemporary interiors, with the attractive red brick facade and leaded casement windows at the front, and private outdoor terraces to the rear of the development. In addition, a reconfiguration of the ground floor retail units provides a contemporary and efficient retail offering.

Estate: The Grosvenor Estate
Status: Completed in May 2013
Architect: Latitude Architects
Structural engineer: Hurst Pierce & Malcolm
M&E engineer: E.A. Pearce
Planning consultant: Gerald Eve
Project manager: Grosvenor
Cost consultant: Thompson Cole
Contractor: Chorus
Interior architecture: Helen Green Design

EAST VILLAGE E20

East Village is a crucial part of the transformation of East London and the latest chapter in the capital's Olympic legacy. The project aims to respond to the critical need for high quality new housing in London and also to act as a future blueprint for modern, sustainable living. East Village is London's newest neighbourhood offering 2,818 high quality homes making a significant impact for housing in London. It offers an array of living options, from one bedroom apartments to four bedroom townhouses, private rental with Get Living London, to shared ownership, intermediate rent and social rent with Triathlon Homes. In addition the new parklands, retail spaces, a world-class education campus and state of the art healthcare facilities for new and existing local communities, mean that this will be a place to live and enjoy for many generations.

Estate: East Village (Get Living London & Triathlon Homes)
Status: Completing in 2013
Masterplanner: Fletcher Priest Architects
Developer: Olympic Delivery Authority (ODA)
Legacy owners: Get Living London and Triathlon Homes
Architects: Allford Hall Monaghan Morris, Applied Landscape Design, Bligh Voller Nield, CF Moller Architects, Denton Corker Marshall, DRMM, DSDHA, Eric Parry Architects, Fletcher Priest Architects, Glenn Howells Architects, Haworth Tompkins, Lifschutz Davidson Sandilands, Niall McLaughlin Architects, Panter Hudspith Architects, Patel Taylor, Penoyre & Prasad, Piercy & Company, PRP, Vogt

119 EBURY STREET SW1W

This project investigates the boundaries of sustainability while maintaining the historic fabric of a Grade II Listed Georgian residential property. The three duplex apartment scheme will test the success of various environmental initiatives over a two-year monitoring programme, including benchmarking against the performance of Grosvenor's standard specification. Initiatives include vacuum glazing, internal wall insulation, 100 per cent low-energy lighting, rain water harvesting and renewable supplies (solar thermal and PV), alongside a fully integrated Building Management Systems (BMS).

Estate: The Grosvenor Estate
Status: Listed Building Consent granted May 2013, currently in design stage, due to complete November 2015
Architect: David Morley Architects
Structural engineer: Hurst Pierce & Malcolm
M&E engineer: Edward Pierce Associates
Planning consultant: Gerald Eve
Project manager: Grosvenor
Cost consultant: Thompson Cole
Contractor: Grangewood Builders

3-10 GROSVENOR CRESCENT SW1X

3-10 Grosvenor Crescent is one of London's premier residential developments and restoration projects. Eight Grade II* listed Regency townhouses have been reconfigured into 15 ultra high end apartments, immaculately restored and returned to their 19th century glory, whilst incorporating the finest elements of contemporary detailing. The apartments include a mix of duplex penthouses, lateral apartments and three- to four-storey grand apartments, which offer private terraces and courtyard gardens. All residents have membership of 19th century Belgrave Square Gardens and 24-hour access to the concierge team.
22 car secure underground parking plots and one separate garage are also included.

Estate: The Grosvenor Estate
Status: Completed in May 2012
Architect: Paul Davis & Partners
Structural engineer: URS
M&E engineer: Arup
Planning consultant & project manager: Grosvenor
Cost consultant: EC Harris
Contractor: Walter Lilly
Interior architecture: Helen Green Design

33 GROSVENOR STREET W1K

This project involves the regeneration and new build development of a Grade II listed building, completing in May 2015. The grand listed rooms will be revitalised through contemporary design and will incorporate a new link as open plan Grade A office to provide 10,376 square feet NIA. As part of the scheme, a brand new residential mews will be built at 2 Three Kings Yard (to the rear of Grosvenor Street) releasing three secure two bedroom prime Mayfair residential apartments.

Estate: The Grosvenor Estate
Status: Starting on site, due to complete May 2015
Architect: Squire and Partners
Structural & M&E engineer: Ramboll
Planning consultant: Gerald Eve
Project manager: Grosvenor
Cost consultant: EC Harris
Contractor: Sir Robert McAlpine

26-28 HALLAM STREET W1W

This conversion of an eight storey commercial property into six high specification flats presented an opportunity to depart from the usual constraints that are seen when working in the listed Georgian and early Victorian properties that are more common to the area. The 1940s Streamline Moderne building now houses a mixed scale of flats, from one-bedroom flats at first floor to family size duplexes across the upper four floors. The building was also extended at roof level creating a unique urban living space and external terrace to capture the stunning views over the Harley Street Conservation Area. Outside, the prominent horizontal bands of glazing were replaced with bronze anodised aluminium double glazed units with an acoustic performance to meet the challenging environment of a noisy traffic junction and ground floor pub.

Estate: The Howard de Walden Estate
Status: Completed in April 2013
Architect: Sonnemann Toon Architects
Structural engineer: Fairhurst GGA
M&E engineer: Prospero Projects Ltd
Contractor: Iconic
Project manager, contract administrator & quantity surveyor:
Howard de Walden Management

122 HARLEY STREET W1G

The existing building is a Grade II listed, six storey Georgian terrace situated on a corner plot with its main elevation to Harley Street. The works comprised general refurbishment of the main house and the refurbishment and extension of a rear annex, replicating the traditional materials of the conservation area. The former transformed the existing mixed-use accommodation into four residential units. High quality living spaces were created utilising the existing volume of the property, employing a light touch when altering existing historic fabric. A new two-storey extension was created for the rear annex forming a three bedroom residence with a small courtyard garden and new dedicated access off the street to the rear.

Estate: The Howard de Walden Estate
Status: Completed in March 2013
MEP engineer: Prospero Projects Ltd
Structural engineer: Fairhurst GGA
Project manager & CDM-C: Nexus Project Services Ltd

2 HYDE PARK SQUARE W2

Hawkins\Brown has recently completed the redevelopment of a 1960s block into high value flats in the Bayswater Conservation Area of Westminster. The existing building was stripped back to its concrete frame and remodeled to create 36 new residential apartments with underground parking. A lightweight rooftop extension has been added to house a large penthouse flat with spectacular views across the West End and Regent's Park. Hawkins\Brown worked closely with the client, Liberty Properties, and agents, Savills, to deliver high quality apartments. The interiors provide the residents with warm oak and limestone finishes, state of the art audio visual and lighting capacities. Each kitchen and bathroom is individually planned to incorporate high-quality contemporary fittings and fixtures.

Estate: The Church Commissioners (Hyde Park Estate)
Status: Completed in January 2013
Developer: Liberty Properties
Architect: Hawkins\Brown
Structural engineer: Price&Myers
M&E engineer: Hurley Palmer Flatt
Planning consultant: Savills
Project manager: Liberty Properties PLC
Cost consultant: MDA Consulting Ltd
Contractor: Pochin Construction

PEABODY AVENUE PIMLICO, SW1V

This designated Conservation Area, a distinctive Victorian estate with its two long opposing rows, has been redeveloped to address the disjointed design left by WWII damage, providing 56 new homes of mixed tenure, new community facilities including a community hall and City Guardians office, and landscape improvements to the whole estate. The design was produced in collaboration with local residents, Westminster City Council and English Heritage, and all new homes feature super-insulation, energy efficient ventilation, water-saving appliances, and double and triple-glazing. Utilising three types of brick, the new buildings work in harmony with the original 19th century material.

Estate: Peabody
Status: Completed in March 2011
Architect: Haworth Tompkins Architects
Contractor: Mansell Construction Services
Structural engineer: Price and Myers
Employers agent: Bristow Johnson
M&E consultant: Max Fordham and Partners
Landscape architect: Coe Design Landscape Architecture

QUADRANT 4 12 SHERWOOD STREET, W1F

Quadrant 4 transforms a 1930s Art Deco Hotel Building off Piccadilly Circus into 38 luxury apartments. The scheme, spread over the top five floors of a nine storey building, removes and reorders the building's upper floors and rear elevation. The existing central lightwell – converted into an internal space with the addition of a new, glazed ceiling – is traversed by a series of bridges, which, in eliminating the need for perimeter corridors, increase the number of through and dual aspect apartments. The ground floors uses of new retail spaces and the existing gym are sensitively rearranged to accommodate the new passenger lift core and upgrade the public realm.

Estate: The Crown Estate
Project status: Stage E - onsite in March 2014, completion in 2015
Development Manager: M3 Consulting
Architect: Allford Hall Monaghan Morris
Structural engineer: Waterman Group
Services engineer: AECOM
Planning consultant: CB Richard Ellis
Heritage consultant: Donald Insall Associates
CDM coordinator: PFB Construction Management Services

19-22 RODMARTON STREET WC1

19 – 22 Rodmarton Street is being developed as part of the Portman Estate's strategic plan to maintain and enhance its properties. Four high-quality, space-efficient and sustainable living spaces (targeting a 4* Code for Sustainable Homes rating) will replace dilapidated mews buildings located within the curtilage of a number of listed buildings. The local street character will be preserved with a modern interpretation of the mews typology, featuring articulated windows and a reinstated roofscape. Internal courtyards and lightwells will be introduced to improve daylight penetration and natural ventilation, and the project pursues a good level of integration between architecture, structure and service design.

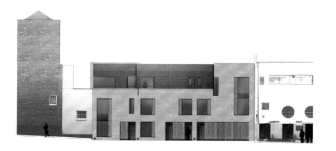

Estate: The Portman Estate
Status: Planning granted April 2013, due to complete in 2015
Architect: Bennetts Associates Architects
Structural engineer: Furness Partnership
M&E engineer: Leonard Engineering Design Associates
Planning consultant: Gerald Eve
Cost consultant: Potter Raper Partnership

RUBICON COURT 3 YORK WAY, N1C

The first homes at King's Cross were completed in summer 2012. Rubicon Court was delivered for King's Cross's affordable housing partner One Housing Group, and provide 117 affordable homes of which 78 are social rented apartments, 15 are supported housing apartments, and 24 are available as shared ownership homes. Almost a third of the apartments are suitable for families - with three or four bedrooms. Designed by PRP Architects, the apartments are arranged in small clusters, allowing communities to develop on each floor. All are designed to meet Lifetime Homes standards. Funding support for Rubicon Court was provided by the Homes and Communities Agency.

Estate: King's Cross (King's Cross Central Limited Partnership)
Status: Completed in July 2012
Client: King's Cross Central Ltd Partnership for One Housing Group
Architect: PRP
Structural & M&E engineer: WSP
Planning Consultant: Argent
Project Manager: King's Cross Central Limited Partnership
Cost Consultant: Davis Langdon (an AECOM company)
Contractor: Carillion

SAXON COURT AND ROSEBERRY MANSIONS 5 YORK WAY, N1C

Designed by Maccreanor Lavington Architects, Saxon Court and Roseberry Mansions are part of the second residential scheme to be delivered at King's Cross. Saxon Court provides 63 social rented apartments and 40 affordable shared ownership homes whilst Roseberry Mansions provides 40 apartments designed for the active elderly. These homes allow older people to live independently while also having access to the care and support services which they may need over time. The buildings overlook the new Cubitt Park and residents have access to courtyards and rooftop gardens. These 143 affordable homes have been delivered for One Housing Group.

Estate: King's Cross (King's Cross Central Limited Partnership)
Status: Completed in October 2012
Architect: Maccreanor Lavington
Structural engineer: Ramboll
M&E engineer: Hoare Lea
Planning consultant: Argent
Project manager: King's Cross Central Limited Partnership
Cost consultant: Davis Langdon (an AECOM company)
Contractor: Carillion

STUDENT RESIDENTIAL BUILDING AT KING'S CROSS KING'S CROSS, N1C

This new student residential building will provide 198 bedrooms, predominantly for use by graduate students attending the Aga Khan University - Institute for the Study of Muslim Civilisations (AKU-ISMC) and the Institute for Ismali Studies (IIS). The scheme is being developed on behalf of the Aga Khan Development Network. The building comprises two 12 storey 'bookend' wings above a ground floor plinth, flanking a central eight-storey element, which is set back from the street. The ground floor offers flexible commercial use while communal roof garden spaces will be provided at first and eighth floors.

Estate: King's Cross (King's Cross Central Limited Partnership)
Date of completion: 2015
Status: Planning granted July 2013
Developer: King's Cross Central Limited Partnership
Development manager: Argent (King's Cross) Ltd
Client: Aga Khan Development Network
Architect: Stanton Williams
Structural engineer: AKT II
M&E engineer: Grontmij

TAPESTRY APARTMENTS 1-5 CANAL REACH, N1C

Designed by award winning Níall McLaughlin Architects, Tapestry is on Canal Reach, adjacent to the Grade II listed Gasholder No. 8 Urban Park and the Regent's Canal. An innovative mixed-use building, Tapestry comprises 129 residential units, the King's Cross Energy Centre, a multi-storey car park, a multi-use games area and retail at ground floor. Tapestry's 95 private apartments range from studios to three bedrooms, including duplex and triplex townhouses set around a private landscaped garden in the sky designed by acclaimed landscape architect Dan Pearson and luxurious penthouses with sweeping views over London. The building's interiors have been intelligently designed by Johnson Naylor using a bespoke palette of quality materials.

Estate: King's Cross (King's Cross Central Limited Partnership)
Status: Planning granted (April 2013), due to complete late 2015
Architects: Niall McLaughlin & Weedon Partnership
Structural engineer: Ramboll UK
M&E engineer: Watermans Building Services
Planning consultants: Argent & CBRE
Project manager: King's Cross Central Limited Partnership
Cost consultants: Davis Langdon (an AECOM company) & Gardner & Theobald
Contractor: Kier
Other key project team members: Dan Pearson Studio, Johnson Naylor, Davis Langdon (an AECOM company), AECOM Fire

NO. 75/76 & NO. 77/78 WIMPOLE STREET W1G

These buildings, treated as two pairs, have been refurbished and modernised with links through party walls respecting the original rooms. The new facade of 77 is developed following studies of the proportions/rhythms of 71-79 Wimpole Street, and is a contemporary interpretation of bay windows, balconies and dormers. 75/76, a Grade II listed matching pair c.1897, have been extended at the rear at floor level, with light wells enclosed with roof lights to fully utilise natural light. Extensions are contemporary in form and detailing. No. 78, also Grade II listed, has been linked to 77 to enable new office spaces, wrapping around a courtyard, to the rear.

Estate: The Howard de Walden Estate
Status: 75/76 due to complete in September 2013 and 77/78 due to complete in January 2014
Architectural team: Soundy Kilaiditi Architects
Project manager: IDC Consult
Structural & geotechnical: Jampel Davison & Bell
M&E engineer: Long & Partners
Quantity surveyor: Jones Lang LaSalle
Contractor: Iconic Build

URBANEST KING'S CROSS CANAL REACH, N1C

The building, including a 27 storey tower, in the north of King's Cross provides high quality, affordable accommodation for over 650 students. It has been delivered by student housing developer, urbanest. The landmark tower, designed by Glenn Howells Architects, houses a range of shared flats with media centres, common rooms, study areas and terraces. Catering facilities are available at street level, with cafés and food stores fronting onto York Way and Canal Street.

Estate: King's Cross (King's Cross Central Limited Partnership)
Status: Completed in July 2013
Client: Urbanest
Architect: Glenn Howells Architects
Structural engineer: Ramboll
M&E engineer: Faber Mansell
Planning consultant: Gerald Eve
Project manager: Urbanest
Cost consultant: MACE/Urbanest
Contractor: Mansell

RETAIL & LEISURE

BARBICAN CINEMA SILK ST, EC2Y

The first new venue to be built since the arts centre's opening 30 years ago, Barbican Cinema is a 'satellite' insertion within the wider listed fabric of the Barbican estate. In response to the bold scale of the brutalist complex and drawing upon the same clear language of AHMM's earlier Barbican reconfiguration projects, the elevations of the former Exhibition Hall – previously opaque and impermeable – are transformed into fully-glazed, active frontages. Accommodating two new cinema screens, a coffee shop and a restaurant, the addition asserts its presence on this prominent street corner at the junction of Beech Street and Whitecross Street. AHMM designed the exteriors only; interior layouts are by cinema specialist designers NBDA.

Estate: The City of London Corporation
Project status: Completed in May 2013
Clients: City of London Corporation & Barbican Centre
Architect: Allford Hall Monaghan Morris
Structural engineer: Furness Partnership
M&E consultant: Crofton Design

THE CADOGAN CAFÉ 9 DUKE OF YORK SQUARE, CHELSEA, SW3

Commissioned through a design competition arranged by Malcolm Reading Consultants, The Cadogan Café by Nex Architecture completes the urban space around the south end of the Duke of York Square. The Cadogan Estate wanted to utilise this popular area to create a landmark mini-destination. The design addressed the complexities of the setting, including an imposing grade II listed wall and busy King's Road. The scheme incorporates inner colonnade glazing which can be retracted to allow free-flowing movement during warm weather, whilst at roof level customers can sit and enjoy the views of the square and its surroundings. The walls are a monocoque construction, employing standard building components and connections, creating form and spatial enclosure and avoiding the need for expensive additional cladding.

Estate: The Cadogan Estate
Status: Design stage, due to complete Spring 2015
Architect and lead consultant: Nex
Structural engineers: AKTII
Environmental engineers: Atelier 10
Cost consultants: Equals
Lighting consultants: DHA Design
Planning consultant: Gerald Eve
Heritage consultant: Donald Insall Associates
Health and safety consultants: PDM Consultants

COAL DROPS KING'S CROS, N1C

With its canalside location, Victorian architecture and new public spaces as a backdrop, the Coal Drops is set to become a unique shopping destination in the capital. Cobbled streets and Victorian brick arches give this new retail quarter a striking and distinct atmosphere, with shops and cafés spilling out onto the streets and public spaces. Free from traffic, the area will be buzzing with street life, quirky boutiques, restaurants, galleries, music venues, street food stalls and more. The old buildings will be sympathetically restored, bringing together their industrial heritage with exciting contemporary design.

Estate: King's Cross (King's Cross Central Limited Partnership)
Status: Outline planning consent granted December 2006
Architect: Lifschutz Davidson Sandilands
Structural engineer: Arup
M&E engineer: Hoare Lea
Planning consultant: Argent
Project manager: King's Cross Central Limited Partnership
Cost consultant: Davis Langdon (an AECOM company)

76 DEAN STREET 76 DEAN STREET AND 5 RICHMOND MEWS, W1D

Recognised as being the second most important Georgian townhouse in Westminster, and the most important in Soho, this Grade II* listed building, originally built in 1732, was gutted by fire in 2009 and has sat empty and open to the elements ever since. Soho Estates acquired the property in 2011 and reached an agreement with Soho House, paving the way to a viable restoration of the property to its former glory including all elements of note internally. In its reincarnation the building will become home to the latest Soho House private members club.

Estate: Soho Estates
Status: Under construction, due to complete September 2014
Architect: soda.
Structural engineer: Price & Myers
M&E engineer: Thornton Reynolds
Planning consultant: Gerald Eve
Project manager: Development Managers Limited
Cost consultant: Gleeds
Contractor: In House Build

52 GLOUCESTER PLACE W1H

This long term vacant Grade II listed Georgian building, fallen into disrepair, has been extensively refurbishment into modern commercial accommodation, offering comfort cooling, new contemporary WCs, kitchenettes and communal kitchen and new lift. Works included structural repair and strengthening, repair and reinstatement of original Georgian decorative features and the reconstruction of the rear extension to improve the lettable floor area. The mid-terrace, built in 1790, is now home to the headquarters of global cosmetics brand Jo Malone.

Estate: The Portman Estate
Status: Completed in April 2012
Architect: Feildon + Mawson
Structural engineer: Furness Partnership
M&E engineer: Leonard Engineering
Cost consultant: Stace QS
Contractor: Richardsons (Nyewood) Ltd

MERCERS' YARD MERCERS' BLOCK C, COVENT GARDEN, WC2H

This urban insertion into Covent Garden seeks to enhance and complement the surrounding urban realm through simple, elegant and very well detailed buildings. A new street is created, making a new link between Mercer & Langley Streets thus connecting it to St. Martin's Courtyard. The scheme also introduces a piazza, allowing an identifiable social courtyard at the heart of the newly accessible site. The retained historic 19th century warehouse will be joined by three new 'warehouse' buildings, each accommodating apartments and ground level shops, bringing life to the new street and piazza.

Estate: The Mercers' Company
Status: Planning pending, due to complete March 2016
Lead consultant & architect: Ian Ritchie Architects Ltd
Structural engineer: Fairhurst GGA
M&E / sustainability engineer: Hoare Lea
Planning consultant: Dp9
Development manager: Hanover Cube

STORE STREET REGENERATION SCHEME 6 STORE STREET, 8 RIDGMOUNT STREET, 28 - 42 STORE STREET, WC1E

Store Street is a mixed-use urban regeneration scheme comprising three distinct elements: a new BREEAM Excellent Office Building at 8 Ridgmount Street, a new restaurant/ retail component on the site of the former Bloomsbury Service Station corner site at 6 Store Street and fourteen retail units and apartments above at 28-42 Store Street. The regeneration strategy has been to attract independent retailers by high quality design, conserving the character of the area and introducing public art, graphic design and enhancements to the public space. A new urban hub has been created which has been cited as an example of high street regeneration by the retail property industry and press.

Estate: The Bedford Estates
Status: Completed in February 2012
Architect: Garnett+Partners LLP
Structural engineer: Mason Navarro Pledge
M&E engineers: Taylor Project Services and E+M Tecnica
Planning consultant: Gerald Eve
Contractors: Chorus Group and Dray Building

SPONSOR & SUPPORTER PROFILES

CLUTTONS

Cluttons is a limited liability partnership of chartered surveyors, founded in 1765. Through our network of offices in the UK, Europe, Middle East, South Africa and the Caribbean, we offer a very wide range of professional property management, agency and consultancy services across the commercial and residential sectors, for both investors and occupiers.

We combine integrity and energy with experience and expertise. Our clients come to Cluttons because of the firm's reputation; they stay because they receive a quality and style of personal service that they cannot find elsewhere.

Cluttons' residential consultancy team offers a full and integrated service to its clients. With unrivalled expertise and knowledge the team provides advice and support across all aspects of the residential sector. Key services include portfolio lettings management, residential investment agency, estate management, valuation consultancy, affordable housing, leasehold enfranchisement and expert witness.

Contact Cluttons LLP, Portman House, 2 Portman Street, London W1H 6DU
Phone 020 7408 1010 **Website** www.cluttons.com

FUTURE\CITY

FUTURE CITY

Futurecity work in an urban context, creating creative neighbourhoods, brokering cultural partnerships and delivering cultural projects from inception to completion. We believe in applying emerging curatorial and cultural models to the urban realm and our approach has helped support the placemaking ambitions of London Estates, including Capital & Counties (Earls Court), Canary Wharf Group (Wood Wharf), Shaftesbury Estate (Carnaby) Crown Estates (St James Market) and the City of London (City Arts Initiative). Elsewhere we are developing ambitious plans for Convoys Wharf, London Dock and Greenwich Peninsula.

In recent years Futurecity have offered over 100 artists opportunities to work on projects of status, impact and scale, recent examples include the 8 new central stations for Crossrail, Mark Wallinger's 50 metre 'White Horse' for Ebbsfleet Valley, Richard Wilson's 76 metre 'Slipstream' for Heathrow's new Terminal 2, an ambitious arts programme for the new Guys Cancer Research Centre and a public art strategy for the newLondon Bridge Station.

Contact 57 Clerkenwell Road, London EC1M 5NG
Phone 020 7407 0500 **Website** www.futurecity.co.uk

SAVILLS

Savills is a leading global real estate service provider listed on the London Stock Exchange. The company, established in 1855, has a rich heritage and a network of over 500 offices and associates throughout the Americas, Europe, Asia Pacific, Africa and the Middle East, employing over 23,000 staff worldwide. Savills advises private and institutional clients seeking to acquire, lease, develop or realise the value of prime residential and commercial property in the World's key locations including London where the firm has an extensive estate management team. The firm also provides corporate finance advice, fund management and a range of property related financial services.

Savills UK operates out of more than 80 offices nationally with in excess of 3,000 staff, covering 15 main business streams and over 150 different service lines. Testimony to the quality of our work, Savills has been the recipient of numerous sector awards including Number 1 Agent for the last 11 years and the Leading Property Superbrand for 4 consecutive years.

Contact Savills, 33 Margaret Street, London W1G 0JD
Phone 020 7499 8644 **Website** www.savills.co.uk

THE BEDFORD ESTATES

The Bedford Estates represents the holdings of the Dukes of Bedford, who have been major landowners in Bloomsbury since 1669. Over half of the Estates' properties are listed. From the original holding of 112 acres, substantial areas were sold during the late 19th and early to mid-20th centuries. Today the Estate covers approximately 30 acres and has approximately 200 properties.

The portfolio comprises a mix of office, educational, hotel, retail and residential uses. Over recent years a considerable proportion of the Estate's properties has been refurbished and upgraded. The combination of preserving heritage assets, ensuring they meet the needs of 21st century occupiers, and nurturing and improving public realm within Bloomsbury, are key drivers for the Estate's long term aspirations.

Contact The Bedford Estates, 29a Montague Street, London WC1B 5BL
Phone 0207 299 8340 **Website** www.bedfordestates.com

BRITISH LAND

British Land is a real estate investment company based in London and listed on the London Stock Exchange. We create value by actively managing, financing and developing prime commercial property to provide the environment in which modern business can thrive.

British Land owns or manages real estate worth £16.9 billion (British Land share £11 billion), with Central London offices comprising 40% of the portfolio. Sustainability is at the core of the business – from community involvement in the planning process, through development, refurbishment and management, the aim is to provide attractive buildings that minimise resource use and meet the needs of occupiers today and tomorrow.

Contact York House, 45 Seymour Street, London W1H 7LX
Phone 020 7486 4466 **Website** www.britishland.com

THE CADOGAN ESTATE

The Cadogan Estate includes 93 acres of Chelsea and Knightsbridge, comprising some of the most fashionable districts of the capital in which to live, work and visit. It is home to some of the most glamorous shopping streets in the world; Sloane Street, Duke of York Square, Sloane Square and parts of King's Road. World class entertainment is provided by the leading concert venue Cadogan Hall, along with the Royal Court Theatre and the Saatchi Gallery.

Cadogan are committed to investing for the long-term success of the area, doing so in a sympathetic way and acting as good neighbours within the community. The Estate includes 3,000 flats, 600 houses, over 300 shops and 500,000 sq ft of office space and has a value of circa £3.9 billion. The family's 300 year stewardship continues in the hands of Chairman, Viscount Chelsea, eldest son of Earl Cadogan.

Contact The Cadogan Estate, 18 Cadogan Gardens, London SW3 2RP
Phone 020 7730 4567 **Website** www.cadogan.co.uk

CANARY WHARF GROUP PLC

Canary Wharf Group plc is an integrated property development, investment and management group of companies. Its flagship business and shopping district, Canary Wharf, has a working population of nearly 100,000 people in a diverse range of sectors for some of the world's leading companies. It has paved the way for the regeneration of London's Docklands. It has helped London and the City consolidate its position at the centre of the business world.

Canary Wharf Group has plans in place to continue to develop Canary Wharf in the coming years. This will be in parallel with other central London developments such as the Shell Centre on the South Bank (in a joint venture with Qatari Diar) and 20 Fenchurch Street in the City of London (in a joint venture with Land Securities).

Contact Canary Wharf Group Plc, One Canada Square, Canary Wharf, London E14 5AB
Website www.canarywharf.com **Twitter** @yourcanarywharf

CAPCO

Capital & Counties Properties PLC ('Capco') is one of the largest listed property companies in central London. Key assets, focused on two estates at Earls Court and Covent Garden, are held directly or through joint ventures. Together they are worth £2.1 billion. Capital & Counties Properties PLC creates value and grows value through a combination of asset management, strategic investment and development.

Contact 15 Grosvenor Street, London W1K 4QZ
Phone 020 3214 9150 **Website** www.capitalandcounties.com

CHURCH COMMISSIONERS OF ENGLAND

The Church Commissioners manage an investment fund of some £5.5 billion, held mainly in a diversified portfolio including equities, real estate and alternative investment strategies. The fund and the obligations attached to it derive from the Commissioners' parent charities of the 18th and 19th centuries, respectively Queen Anne's Bounty and the Ecclesiastical Commissioners, which were set up to improve the incomes and housing of clergy and to extend their ministry into new urban areas. The Commissioners' work today supports the Church of England as a Christian presence in every community.

Contact Church Commissioners of England, Church House, Great Smith Street, London SW1P 3AZ
Phone 0207 898 1000 **Website** www.churchofengland.org

CITY OF LONDON CORPORATION

The City of London is a uniquely diverse organisation with three main aims: to support and promote the City as the world leader in international finance and business services; to provide high quality local services and policing for the Square Mile; and to provide valued services to London and the nation as a whole. Within the organisation the City Surveyor's Department manages commercial property with a value in excess of £2bn. As part of the City Corporation's service the City Property Advisory Team (CPAT) acts as a facilitator and adviser between the City of London Departments, City businesses and the property industry.

Contact City of London Corporation, Local Government, City Surveyor's Department, Guildhall, London EC2P 2EJ
Phone 020 7332 3496 **Website** www.cityoflondon.gov.uk

THE CROWN ESTATE

The Crown Estate is a diverse property business valued at £8.1 billion. All of our net surplus (profit) goes to the Treasury for the benefit of the nation. In our Urban Portfolio, we are specialist owners and managers in two key areas: the West End of London, and in prime retail property across the UK.

Dynamic asset management is the hallmark of the work we do. We own extensive prime assets on Regent Street and in St James's, and on a regional portfolio that stretches from Wales and the West Country to the north-east of England and Scotland. Under the Crown Estate Act we have no fresh sources of capital, nor can we borrow. Consequently we operate a business model based on the effective recycling of existing capital and increasingly, the formation of strategic partnerships. We are part of a number of joint venture property partnerships across the UK.

Contact 16 New Burlington Place, London W1S 2HX
Phone 020 7851 5050 **Website** www.thecrownestate.co.uk

EAST VILLAGE

East Village is London's newest neighbourhood on the doorstep of the Queen Elizabeth Olympic Park and at the heart of the new E20 postcode. What was the former London 2012 Athletes' Village has been transformed into a vibrant new neighbourhood, delivering high-quality new homes for individuals, couples and families. East Village offers a range of homes to suit everyone - from one-bedroom apartments to four-bedroom townhouses with a choice of private rental homes with Get Living London, and both affordable rental or purchase with Triathlon Homes. Along with delivering essential new homes for Londoners, East Village will also create 27 hectares of new parklands and open space, new retail space, a world-class education campus and state of the art healthcare facilities for new residents and the existing local community to enjoy.

Contact East Village, 5 Celebration Avenue, London E20 1BD
Website www.eastvillagelondon.co.uk

THE EYRE ESTATE

The Eyre family purchased a farm of 500 acres in St John's Wood in 1733. In 1794 a masterplan was produced which was adapted a number of times. Commencing in 1809, under strict design control, houses were built on land leased to developers. The first garden suburb of approximately 1,500 houses completed in the mid 1800s. Large parts of the estate have now been sold off, originally to finance further development but later to accommodate death duties and confiscation with compensation under the Leasehold Reform Act. Control of the Estate is now limited owing to these sales.

Today the Eyre Estate comprises the remaining part of the original estate which includes ground leased houses, blocks of flats, regulated tenants and AST's, plus a portfolio of large refurbished houses let on short leases, and, from proceeds of sales, commercial properties throughout the UK.

Contact The Eyre Estate, 25 Woronzow Road, London NW8 6AY

GROSVENOR

Grosvenor is a privately owned property group active in some of the world's most dynamic cities. Grosvenor Britain & Ireland's strategy emphasises the creation and management of successful places. The core portfolio comprises 300 acres of Mayfair and Belgravia in London and ownership and active management of the London estate remains at the heart of Grosvenor Britain & Ireland's strategy. Investment assets comprise the largest part of its portfolio. Grosvenor Britain & Ireland also undertakes development across London, and in selected city centres around the UK. As at 31 December 2012, Grosvenor Britain & Ireland had assets under management of £4.8bn.

Grosvenor has an active redevelopment and refurbishment programme that invests in its historical properties and creates exceptional homes for modern living, the most recent example being 65 Duke Street in Mayfair.

Contact Grosvenor, 70 Grosvenor Street, London W1K 3JP
Phone 0207 408 0988 **Website** www.grosvenor.com

THE HOWARD DE WALDEN ESTATE

With direct ties to the area which date back to 1708, the Howard de Walden Estate owns, manages and leases out the majority of the 92 acres of real estate within Marylebone: from Marylebone High Street in the west to Portland Place in the east and from Wigmore Street in the south to Marylebone Road in the north. The Estate's portfolio incorporates over 850 properties, valued at more than £2.5bn and accommodating in excess of 2,000 tenants. Consisting of both modern developments and some of London's most beautiful Georgian and Victorian buildings, it includes office and residential accommodation, the diverse and distinctive retail community on and around Marylebone High Street, and the renowned Harley Street medical area. The Estate's aim is to carefully manage the evolution of each of these sectors while maintaining the character, heritage and strength of community that make Marylebone such a unique part of central London.

Contact The Howard de Walden Estate, 23 Queen Anne Street, London W1G 9DL
Phone 020 7580 3163 **Website** www.hdwe.co.uk

King's Cross

KING'S CROSS CENTRAL LIMITED PARTNERSHIP

King's Cross is being developed by the King's Cross Central Limited Partnership. The partnership is the single land owner at King's Cross, making development and delivery easier. It brings together three groups:

- Argent King's Cross Limited Partnership: Backed by Argent LLP, one of the UK's best respected property development companies and Hermes Real Estate on behalf of the BT Pension Scheme.
- London & Continental Railways Limited: A UK Government-owned property company. Its primary focus is the regeneration projects at King's Cross and The International Quarter, Stratford City.
- DHL Supply Chain: A world-class provider of supply chain solutions.

Contact Granary Building, 1 Granary Square off Goods Way, London N1C 4AA
Phone 020 3664 0200 **Website** www.kingscross.co.uk

LONDON LEGACY DEVELOPMENT CORPORATION

The London Legacy Development Corporation is responsible for the regeneration legacy from the London 2012 Games including overall responsibility for the Park, ownership of the permanent venues and development powers.

The Legacy Corporation is creating a vibrant and dynamic new quarter of London with Queen Elizabeth Olympic Park at its heart. The Park will be like nowhere else in London; a unique destination for visitors, businesses and residents alike. 6,800 homes will be built in five new neighbourhoods with new schools, health centres, nurseries, playgrounds, shops, businesses and commercial districts bringing 8,000 new jobs to the area. The Park will help to transform east London and generate benefits for local people by providing a catalyst for change.

Contact Level 10, One Stratford Place, Montfichet Road, London E20 1EJ
Phone 020 3288 1800 **Website** www.londonlegacy.co.uk, www.QueenElizabethOlympicPark.co.uk

LONDON METROPOLITAN ARCHIVES (LMA)

London Metropolitan Archives (LMA) is home to an extraordinary range of documents, images, maps, films and books about London. It is the largest local authority record office in the United Kingdom, providing access to 105 km of archives. This material dates from 1067 to the present day and covers every imaginable subject. Collections which cover the development of London's estates are particularly strong, especially those of the London County Council, Greater London Council and City of London Corporation for the 20th century.

Offering a wide selection of talks, guided tours, film screenings, exhibitions and other events, LMA is free to use and open to everyone. Whether you're tracing your family history or researching any aspect of the capital's history, if you're interested in London or Londoners, LMA is the place to visit.

Contact 40 Northampton Road, London EC1R 0HB
Phone 020 7332 3820 **Website** www.cityoflondon.gov.uk/lma

THE MERCERS' COMPANY

The Mercers' Company is the Premier Livery Company of the City of London and has over 700 years of documented history. Livery Companies originated in London's medieval trade guilds and the Mercers' originally traded luxury fabrics. Nowadays the Company, and/or its associated charitable trusts manage a network of almshouses and other homes for the elderly; makes substantial grants to support education, general welfare, church and faith and arts and heritage; and is involved with the running of 17 schools. The Company funds its activities from income derived from its investments, mainly property in London's West End and the City. This includes St Martin's Courtyard in Covent Garden, a mixed use development surrounding a new public space. In the City the Company jointly owns the Royal Exchange with the City Corporation.

Contact The Mercers' Company, Mercers' Hall, Ironmonger Lane, London EC2V 8HE
Website www.mercers.co.uk

PEABODY

Peabody is one of London's oldest and largest housing associations, founded in 1862 by American banker and philanthropist George Peabody to "ameliorate the condition of the poor and needy in this great metropolis". Peabody has a reputation for architectural quality, and our original pre-1900 homes, many of which are Grade II listed, have stood the test of time. Today we own or manage around 20,000 properties, providing homes for more than 55,000 people. Operating only in London, we manage a range of tenures, including social housing, leasehold, shared ownership, supported housing, keyworker accommodation and commercial units. We also have an ambitious development and regeneration programme to meet the growing housing needs of London. As well as bricks and mortar, we provide a wide range of community programmes for our residents and neighbourhoods.

Contact 45 Westminster Bridge Road, London SE1 7JB
Phone 020 7021 4444 **Website** www.peabody.org.uk

THE PORTMAN ESTATE

The Portman Estate, covering 110 acres in Marylebone, dates back to the 16th century. The London Estate today comprises the area from Edgware Road to beyond Baker Street and from Oxford Street to Crawford Street in the north. The typology of the Estate is divided equally between residential, commercial and retail/hotel uses in order to ensure a robust and diverse portfolio. The Estate has more recently invested considerably in the refurbishment and upgrading of its properties to enhance the quality of its direct stock. Work continues with a programme of £140 million for the next 5 years. Major developments in Portman Square and Edgware Road are indicative of the continuing demand in the West End, as is the case for Baker Street which represents the Estate's commercial heart. Meanwhile, the vibrant retail districts of Portman Village and Chiltern Street add a local boutique flavour.

Contact Ground Floor, 40 Portman Square, London W1H 6LT
Phone 020 7563 1400 **Website** www.portmanestate.co.uk

SHAFTESBURY PLC

Shaftesbury PLC

Formed in 1986 and listed on the London Stock Exchange in 1987, Shaftesbury PLC has followed a consistent strategy since the early 1990s of investing only in the heart of London's West End. Its concentration of world-class historic and cultural attractions together with an unrivalled variety of shopping and leisure choices attract huge numbers of domestic and international visitors. It is also an important location for businesses, particularly those in the media, creative and IT industries, and a popular place to live. Shaftesbury's wholly-owned portfolio, which extends to 13 acres of freeholds, comprises over 1.6 million sq ft of commercial and residential accommodation concentrated in Carnaby, Covent Garden (Seven Dials, Opera Quarter, Coliseum, St Martin's Courtyard), Chinatown, Soho and Charlotte Street.

Contact Pegasus House, 37/43 Sackville Street, London W1S 3DL
Phone 020 7333 8118 **Website** www.shaftesbury.co.uk

SOUTH KENSINGTON ESTATES

South Kensington Estates Ltd (SKE) is a privately owned property investment company which manages its own portfolio of around 400 properties, located in South Kensington and Brompton Road. The company was set up in 1997 to invest in and develop the portfolio with a view to restoring and recovering an area of London known for its cultural heritage.

The goal of the company is to build a thriving portfolio which is sustainable both in environmental and financial terms over the long-term. As custodians of the property in South Kensington and Brompton, SKE invests significant amounts in upgrading the stock and improving the locality. SKE offices are based on the doorstep of the managed properties. Developing strong relationships with local stakeholder groups is very important to the company philosophy, whether that be local residents, businesses, educational or cultural institutions.

Contact South Kensington Estates, Alfred House, 23-24 Cromwell Place, London SW7 2LD
Phone 020 7761 6420 **Website** www.ske.org

SOHO ESTATES LIMITED

Soho Estates was started by the late Paul Raymond. It was originally conceived as an investment company and Mr Raymond often said that he would only buy properties that he could walk to. Over the years, Soho Estates has continued to expand its holdings within Soho and now also has significant holdings in Leicester Square.

The management team understands the 'village' in which we operate and reacts accordingly. We understand the requirements of our tenants and have helped in times of recession to maintain our cash flow and keep the small businesses of Soho thriving, whilst also helping some businesses to grow into major concerns. The Board is now embarking on an exciting period of development and refurbishment in the area and looking forward to "keeping Soho's Soul" alive for future generations.

Contact Soho Estates Limited, Portland House, 12-13 Greek Street, London W1D 4DL
Phone 020 7534 3333 **Website** www.sohoestates.co.uk

Credits

This book is published by NLA to accompany the NLA exhibition Great Estates: How London's landowners shape the city

Researcher
Sarah Yates

Curator
Peter Murray

Design
Niten Patel
Martin Page

Editor
Catherine Staniland

Co-ordinator
Jenine Hudson

With special thanks to:
Stephen Andrews, Toby Anstruther, Rosemary Ashton, Melanie Backe-Hansen, Sir Nicholas Bacon, Tim Bacon, Peter Bennett, Claire Bennie, Gillie Bexson, Brian Bickell, Faye Bird, Polly Bradshaw, Adam Bray, Julian Briant, Stuart Buss, Tim Butler, Mark Chapman, Stephanie Chapman, Anna Clemenson, Malcolm Cohen, Stuart Corbyn, Karen Crawshaw, Richard Crook, Jessica Curtis, Sarah Jane Curtis, Hugo Day, William Donger, Alison Duke, Robert Evans, Richard Everett, Ellie Farrell, Duncan Ferguson, Kathryn Firth, Hilary Forrester, Oliver French, Lauren Geisler, Tom Greenall, Damian Greenish, Nick Hall-Stride, Jenny Hancock, Geoff Harris, Nigel Hughes, Duncan Innes, Ted Johnson, Mike Jones, Kristian Kaminski, Jonathan Kendall, Rosanna Lawes, David Lockyer, Simon Loomes, John E Major, Marc McConnell, Mark McKeown, Pat Molyneux, Will Montague, Bill Moore, Ben Murphy, Cathryn Pender, Matthew Pinsent, Jodie Playfoot, Nancy Pound, Richard Powell, Shona Price, Anna Rakitina, Antony Rifkin, Mark de Rivaz, Jane Ruddell, Andrew Saint, Deborah Saunt, Bill Scarborough, Marcus Scrace, Hugh Seaborn, Toby Shannon, David Shaw, Andrew Sissons, Stephen Snead, Jennifer Squire, Andrew Stebbings, Phil Thompson, Christine Wagg, Katharine Walsh, Ed Watson, Laura Whyte, Stephen Wilcox, Adam Wiles, Nigel Williams

NLA team:
Peter Murray (Chairman); Nick McKeogh (Chief executive); Debbie Whitfield (Director); Bill Young (Financial controller); Catherine Staniland (Programme director); Jessame Cronin (Programme manager); Stephanie Ellers (Programme manager – logistics); Jenine Hudson (Exhibition co-ordinator); Danielle Rowland (Event director); Michelle Haywood (Events & marketing co-ordinator); Claire Hopkins (Business development director); Zoe Couch (Account director); Anna Cassidy (Account manager); Lauren Bennett (Membership co-ordinator)

Further reading

The Survey of London

Essential reading for anyone with a general or research interest in London's estates is the Survey of London. Founded in the 1890s, it produces detailed architectural and topographical studies of central London and the inner suburbs, the area administered (pre-1965) by the London County Council. Each volume or set of volumes covers one parish or borough, and the 50th volume will be published in late 2013. There are also 17 volumes in the Monograph Series, which covers notable sites and buildings. Almost all volumes are now in a fully searchable form online on the Institute of Historical Research's British History Online website following a four-year project funded by English Heritage to make them freely available. For a full list and links to online volumes see:

www.english-heritage.org.uk/professional/research/buildings/survey-of-london/survey-of-london-online/

Other publications

Peter Ackroyd, *London: The Biography*
(Vintage, new edition, 2001)

Tony Aldous, *The Illustrated London News Book of London's Villages*
(Secker & Warburg, 1980)

Rosemary Ashton, *Victorian Bloomsbury*
(Yale University Press, 2012)

Peter Barber, *London: A History in Maps*
(British Library Publishing, 2012)

Mireille Galinou, *Cottages and Villas: The Birth of the Garden Suburb*
(Yale University Press, 2010)

Joyce Godber, *The Harpur Trust, 1552–1973*
(The Harpur Trust, Bedford, 1973)

Shirley Green, *Who Owns London?*
(Weidenfeld & Nicolson, 1986)

Simon Jenkins, *Landlords to London: A Story of a Capital and its Growth*
(Faber & Faber 2012; facsimile reprint of the original 1975 edition)

Todd Longstaffe-Gowan, *The London Square: Gardens in the Midst of Town*
(Yale University Press, 2012)

Donald J Olsen, *The Growth of Victorian London*
(Penguin, 1979)

Nick Owen, *A Long and Winding Road – The Story of John Lyon's Charity*
(John Lyon's Charity, 2013)

Roy Porter, *London: A Social History*
(Penguin, 1994, new edition 2000)

Ben Weinreb, Christopher Hibbert, Julia Keay and John Keay, *The London Encyclopedia*
(Macmillan, third edition, 2010)

David Wixon & Alison Graham, *The Berkeley Square Estate: Expressions
of Elegance and Excellence*
(Lancer Property Asset Management Limited, 2008)

John Summerson, *Georgian London*
(Yale University Press, revised edition, 2003, originally published 1945)

Index

Index

Index